D0815329

THE AFTERLIFE HANDBOOK

Other books by Michael Powell

101 People You Won't Meet in Heaven
Behave Yourself!
Body Tricks
Express Yourself!

THE AFTERLIFE HANDBOOK
A Travel Guide to Your Final Destination

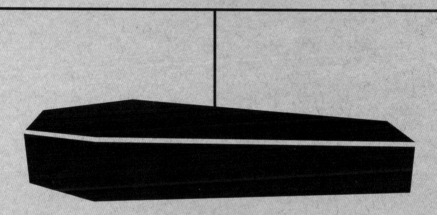

MICHAEL POWELL

The Lyons Press
Guilford, Connecticut
An Imprint of The Globe Pequot Press

DISCLAIMER TO FELLOW TRAVELLERS

To the full extent permissible by law the author and publishers shall have no liability for any damage or loss (including, without limitation, financial loss, loss of religious faith, loss of body fluids, coffee through the nose, trapped wind, or consequential loss), however it arises, resulting from the use of or inability to use this book or from any action or decision taken as a result of reading or not reading it. This book is intended as a work of humorous fiction, and as such it may offend those with a highly over-developed sense of their own importance. In the unlikely event that you experience symptoms of sanctimonious indignation while reading the material contained herein, you are advised to get over yourself, and try to spread love and joy instead of bumming everyone out with your moral outrage. If you think your God might also take offense, then remember that this is still only your opinion, and that He/She doesn't need you fighting His/Her battles on His/Her behalf, since He/She is perfectly capable of sticking up for Himself/Herself.

CONTENTS

INTRODUCTION

Despite being a place beyond our powers of mortal comprehension, the afterlife has much to offer the deceased person—panoramic scenery, fine culture, neoclassical architecture, burning fires, ceaseless torture, or eternal bliss (depending on your destination).

Whether you are a believer or atheist, Satanist and/or Scientologist, this reference bible could save your life. Well, actually, it's probably too late for that, but it will make your afterlife a less confusing and more enjoyable experience. You'll find yourself referring to it time and time again, until your number is up. It's a must-buy for anyone with even the slightest chance of kicking the bucket in the near or distant future—guess that means you.

This guide contains troves of information about cashing in your chips, crossing the Great Divide, and freeing the spirit—everything from how to behave at the Pearly Gates to using containers and hanging baskets to transform even the smallest cloud into your own miniature paradise.

We want you to have the time of your afterlife, and with this book it can be an experience beyond your wildest dreams by helping you prepare for the highs and lows, pleasure and pitfalls, of answering the final call.

Many people who have near-death experiences report reaching a "point of no return" where they had to face the difficult choice to go forward or backward. Having

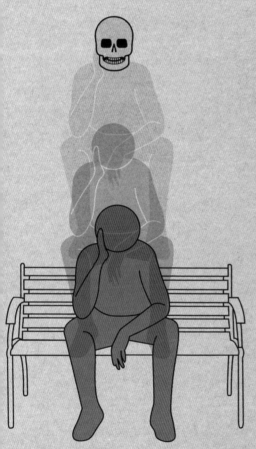

made the decision to return to his or her earthly body, nearly all of them appear to conquer their fear of death.

You may be facing a similar dilemma right now as you shelter from the rain on a Sunday afternoon, leafing through these pages and trying to decide whether to splash some cash and explore the farthest reaches of the Stygian shores or go home and eat some grilled cheese.

The choice is yours, but we sincerely hope you continue to walk toward the light . . .

STARTING THE JOURNEY

At the end of Ridley Scott's sci-fi masterpiece, Blade Runner, *Dutch dreamboat Roy Batty sits bare-chested in the rain during the final moments of his short life and reflects on the human condition. He observes with rueful dignity how his unique life experiences, "all those moments" will be "lost . . . in time like . . . [clears his throat] tears in rain. . . . time to die."*

It's probably the most moving death in the history of the world, even if you include those of both Jesus Christ and Old Yeller. Death comes to us all; whether we are a sophisticated biologically-engineered humanoid or a lop-eared old hound, none of us can cheat the Grim Reaper (except maybe Keith Richards). Death is the essential condition of life, something of which both Roy and Jesus were keenly aware, and Old Yeller was blissfully ignorant, until Travis shot him in the head.

So, in order to get busy living, you'd better get busy learning how to go belly up and ready yourself for the Big Beyond. Even if you are an atheist, to get the most out of this guidebook, you must be prepared to open yourself up to the possibility that there really is something beyond the final curtain. We appreciate that this will take you way outside your comfort zone, push envelopes that you didn't even know existed—snazzy pearlescent paper ones with gold foil and a water repellant coating—and ultimately challenge you to face the possibility that all that smug religious glop may be true.

It's a stiff challenge to make such a profound mind shift when you have spent your life up to now dealing with "facts," and have grounded your "reality" in certainties like how a guy's beard grows faster when he anticipates sex or the impossibility of licking your own elbow. What's not to like about facts? They help us to tame the great unknown, allow us to pass exams, and occasionally to noodle out a hint of what the hell is going on in this vapid trudge towards the grave. Facts are great, but what do you think offers the greater comfort: knowing that the penalty for cracking one off in Indonesia is decapitation, or that your soul will live on beyond your death?

If you are still reluctant to believe in something for which there is no empirical evidence, then you may take comfort that scientists already have proof that a form of consciousness carries on after the body and brain have died: He's called Dick Cheney.

Preparing for death

After centuries of debate, religion, science, and philosophy now agree that the experience we call death can be pinned down to the precise moment when medical fees are replaced by funeral expenses. The body completes its natural process of shutting down and the soul leaves the physical plane to begin its journey to the afterlife.

People who have had a near-death experience often report seeing a bright light and a long tunnel. Tunnels are hardwired into the circle of life: We come into this world down a long fleshy tunnel, and nine months later we squeeze through another one, covered in slime and buffeted by the contractions of a mother's uterus. Many of us spend two hours in a subway tunnel every day of our working lives. It seems fitting that we should leave this world by yet another tunnel.

Judgment Day

A recent study from the Barna Research Group of Ventura, California, showed that 80 percent of Americans believe in an afterlife of some sort, 10 percent are uncertain, and 10 percent believe that there is no life after death. Approximately 76 percent believe that Heaven exists, but only 71 percent believe there is such a thing as Hell.

However, most of us do not expect to be the ones that get sent to Hell: Just one-half of 1 percent think they're heading there after death and nearly two-thirds of Americans believe they will go to Heaven. Even more alarming, 72 percent of them supported the Iraq War, while only 4 percent are aware that Canada is the largest foreign supplier of crude oil to the U.S.

Well, my poor deluded friends, it's time for a reality check.

When you reach the light at the end of the tunnel, you will see a white picket fence bordering a serene and beautifully-lit land-

scape. Don't start celebrating, though, because you haven't reached paradise just yet. You are in fact standing in a huge celestial sorting pen, a metaphysical holding area where you will be issued a space blanket and an isotonic drink while God and the Devil play "Spanish Train" on Guitar Hero III. The stakes couldn't be higher: human souls. [Insert Dr. Evil laughter here.]

This is where you will be called to account. Here the "sheep" are separated from the "goats." You will be asked to strip to your underwear and step gingerly onto the scales for the final reckoning, so that your good deeds can be balanced against the bad ones. As it says in the Qur'an, "actions as small as a grain of mustard seed shall be weighed out," although you can still cheat a bit by leaning forward.

Finally, after due deliberation if it's still too close to call, your fate will be decided on the toss of a coin. Heads it's wings, tails it's tails. Unfair, perhaps, but there you have it: Einstein was wrong— God does play dice.

Reincarnation

At this juncture if you are a Buddhist, Hindu, Sikh, or Jain you will most likely be sent back to earth to be reborn in another body. This isn't as desirable as it may seem. The Buddhists have a word for this endless round of being born again and again, chained to this ruined earth like a dog in a trailer park: They call it "Samsara," which means, "Oh crap. Here we go again." Samsara is associated with suffering and is the antithesis of Nirvana (the Seattle-based grunge rock band).

In the same way that conscientious objectors must register before the outbreak of war to be excused from national service, you can't suddenly convert to a reincarnation religion to escape Hell. However, if you are truly

repentant about your bad deeds, the slate may be wiped clean by the redeeming power of love. Redemption, after all, is the message of so many of the world's greatest parables (think: the Vineyard, the Prodigal Son, and Billy Madison).

The Hindu holy book, the *Bhagavad Gita*, compares rebirth to changing your clothes. When a person's body wears out, he leaves it in an untidy heap on the bathroom floor (just like Elvis did) and puts on a new one. As punishment, you may be reborn as an animal or a realtor, but being born as a human is best, because it brings you closer to salvation, plus you get to own a gun. However, take note: The exponential growth in human population during the last century seems to suggest that more and more animals are moving up the food chain by leading exemplary lives. That's a sobering lesson for us humans.

"AIM AT HEAVEN AND YOU WILL GET EARTH THROWN IN. AIM AT EARTH AND YOU GET NEITHER."

—C. S. Lewis

DESTINATION: HEAVEN

Well, here you are. You're six feet deep in the cold, hard ground, or maybe your ashes have been scattered to the four winds, and your astral spirit, your soul, your essence, has finally arrived in Heaven.

First off, congratulations on reaching paradise! High five. Pat yourself on the back (but be careful not to damage your wings). Clearly either you have been a moral beacon to everyone who has had the pleasure of your company, or

you're so damn cute you crap kittens. God can't resist a pure soul or a pretty face since we are all made in His image (apart from John Dolittle and Tom DeLay).

Now you may think you know all about Heaven from reading the Bible, or that you know all about the Bible by watching *The Omen*, but the afterlife is still what Shakespeare called, "the undiscovered country, from whose bourn no traveler returns." In other words, your opinions are as valid as the Pope's. We are sure you'll be bursting with questions when you arrive.

One of the first things people are literally dying to know is "Am I in Heaven?" The thing about Heaven is you shouldn't have to ask; it ought to be self-evident, and if you need to ask you probably aren't in it. Anyway, you'll soon get a clue from the faces (smiles or smirks), the clothes (silk or leather), and the state of the toilets.

Don't be afraid to ask questions, no matter how silly they are, because there are no stupid questions, only stupid people. And ugly people. Stupid, ugly people. (Thank God you won't find any of them here.) Only kidding—Heaven has more than its fair share of oddballs, but it's what's on the inside that counts, and paradise wouldn't be half as much fun without some Ugly Betties to raise the collective IQ.

HOLY FAQ!

We've tried to anticipate some of your initial concerns by giving answers to many of the most common questions that new arrivals often ask. Some of them are moral conundrums that have engaged philosophers and scholars for centuries, others are more practical, and quite a few are about aardvarks (the natural predator of ants, which form the greatest population in Heaven both numerically and by weight). We feel it only right that their interests are properly represented.

What does "aardvark" mean?
Its name means "earth pig" but it's not related to the pig.

Can I smoke in Heaven?
There is no designated smoking section in Heaven because you can light up anywhere. So far, nobody from the anti-smoking lobby has made it into Heaven, since by definition, not smoking is Hell, and Heaven wouldn't be Heaven if you couldn't smoke there.

God knows that a cigarette is the best buddy a person can have, and that if angels didn't smoke, there wouldn't be any stars. Every time an angel flicks one of their dying butts into the air, someone on earth gets to make a wish. Each cigarette tastes as sweet as the first one of the day.

Smoking here makes your breath and clothes smell amazing while making you look cooler than Joe Camel ever did at all times, even while you're coughing up a lung. God loves smokers; that's why cigarettes are still one of the best ways to shorten your life.

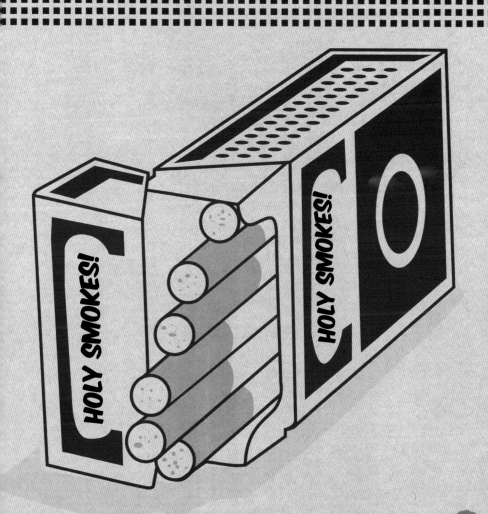

How long is an aardvark's tongue?

The tongue is eighteen inches in length, thin, and sticky. It is perfect for lapping ants up.

Did God really create the world in seven days?

He did it in six days and nights while living on cola and Hershey bars. On the seventh day he went home to discover that his girlfriend had left him.

Why did God create man?

The doctrine of God's Aseity asserts that He doesn't need anything, so He didn't create Adam and Eve to give him companionship, nor did He create them to be a kind of janitor-couple to take care of the earth (although He did tell Adam to name the animals and to tend the garden), so there must be another reason.

To answer this question it is necessary to look forward to the Declaration of Independence: "We hold these truths to be self-evident, that all men are created equal, that they are endowed by their Creator with certain unalienable Rights, that among these are Life, Liberty, and the pursuit of Happiness."

The Founding Fathers knew the answer. It's simple: God created man to establish America.

However, it begs the question, if these are our unalienable rights, why did God create Hell? (For an answer, see page 104.)

What will I look like?

Many theologians attest that in the afterlife we are disembodied entities and that we leave our earthly bodies behind to become pure soul. However, since all souls look kind of the same—small pulsating balls of bright light—it is very difficult to recognize friends and family, as well as to do the simplest of tasks such as make a cup of coffee or send a text message. For the sake of convenience, everyone resembles a more ideal-

21

ized version of their earthly selves: bald people have more hair, short people grow a few inches, and glamour models have believable boob jobs. All fat people become slinky and irresistible pieces of ass (curiously not one person from the "proud to be fat" brigade has ever objected to this).

Can rich people get into Heaven?

Jesus famously said that it is easier for a rich man to pass a camel than get into Heaven. The Bible is very clear on the subject of treasure in Heaven. In Mark 10:21, when the rich man asks Jesus what he must do to inherit eternal life, Jesus replies, "Go, sell everything you have and give to the poor, and you will have treasure in Heaven."

The rich man went away devastated because, before eBay, selling all your stuff was a real drag, and he just didn't have the time to list everything in the want ads or organize a garage sale.

What's the weather like?

The climate is tailored to each individual's preference. It isn't unusual to see someone walking underneath their own thunderstorm or basking beneath a midday sun, and there are always the indecisive types who choose a light drizzle. You can't get sunburned in Heaven, but you can still get tan lines.

Do aardvarks get along with warthogs?

Not really. Warthogs eat baby aardvarks.

Will I still have to wax my bikini line?

Since pubic hair is the best sort of hair, it grows ten times faster in Heaven, which is a boon for Eastern Europeans. However, if you prefer to be smooth, then you should probably make a back-crack-and-sack wax part of your twice-daily routine. You might think that having your pubes growing exponentially is your own private hell, but it's a small price to pay for all the other luxuries, and it's much less of an inconvenience than burning in a lake of boiling sulfur.

Will I have to play the harp?

This myth was created by the writers of the Old Testament. They conceived the idea of angels playing the most perfect musical instrument imaginable at that time—which, in those days, was the harp. Today, angels are expected to reach a basic level of proficiency on lead guitar, though not on a real one. We're talking Rock Band and a plastic controller. After a few days' practice you'll be ready to play battle mode against Jimi Hendrix.

Are the streets of Heaven made of gold?

Here is another classic example of how we wrongly attribute contemporary human values to Heaven. Humankind perceives gold to be one of its most valuable commodities, but pure gold is vulgar and way too soft for road construction. The roads here are built from a mixture of aggregate and recycled household waste which locks in the carbon dioxide to reduce Heaven's carbon wingprint. Cars are banned, so after floating and teleportation, rickshaws are the third most popular form of transport.

Where will I live?

Most angels live on clouds which offer a basic level of comfort, though nearly all of them have humidity issues. You can often snap up a bargain while the cloud is in the development phase (when rising air is being cooled beyond its saturation point).

Technically, you can live anywhere you want. However, if you are a Jehovah's Witness you will be sent to the remotest corner of Heaven, where you and 143,999 of your deluded friends can spend your immortal life believing you are the only ones who made it, while everyone else enjoys the party without you.

Did God really hide all those fossils?

Creationists believe that God hid lots of fossils to fool us into thinking that the earth is millions of years old and that we are descended from apes. Unfortunately, they are spectacularly wrong; evolution is right on the money, since in olden times God was too busy sending plagues of locusts and smiting people to find the time to hide bones. Plus, he never thought for a moment that people would take Genesis so seriously (especially Phil Collins). However, you'd think the Creationists would be satisfied to reach Heaven and find that God exists. But no—they still won't accept that they are wrong even when God lays it on the line.

Do pets go to Heaven?

This question has always troubled theologians, because it throws up the issue of salvation, and whether or not animals have souls and are worthy of redemption. But you can also look at it another way. When you imagine Heaven, is it devoid of everything but "human" life, or do you think it is filled with bird song, animals, and all the other wonders of God's creation? Put it like that and it's much easier to say, "Yes, of course there are animals in Heaven." Besides, if there were no animals, what would we eat?

What is a healthy weight for an aardvark?

Between one hundred and one hundred seventy pounds.

Will there be marriage in Heaven?

Whenever two people are perfect for each other, it is said that their union is a "match made in Heaven," which is curious, since monogamy is no big deal here. Eternity really can feel like a long time when you have to wake up next to the same person every day until Hell freezes over. Cohabiting is more in order, although casual sex is discouraged: You should always give it your full attention.

Gay partnerships are more than welcome, since God seemed pretty pissed when Adam had sex with Eve (maybe he was jealous?), Jesus was never specific when he said, "Love thy neighbor," and Sodom and Gomorrah were destroyed because of the inhospitality of their inhabitants (Matthew 10:14-15) rather than their sexual orientation.

Will we have sex?

If you aren't married, then yes, lots of it. However, it is still a matter of personal choice, although those who devoted their lives to celibacy on earth are encouraged to continue since this tends to stop them breeding more fanatics.

Will we feel sorrow for those in Hell?

This is one of the most perplexing theological paradoxes: presumably only those with a highly developed sense of empathy and compassion get into Heaven, but Heaven is supposed to involve a complete absence of suffering. However, if compassionate people feel sorrow for those in Hell, their own happiness will be tainted. How happy can you really be in Heaven if you feel the pain of all the lost souls trapped in the torments of Hell?

We believe that it must be God's will that some people go to Hell, because if He wanted a certain person to be forgiven, He could step in and make it happen. If He can't do this, then this would mean He wasn't all-powerful; if it's Satan's choice, then this implies that either God is less powerful than Satan, or He is happy for some sinners not to be forgiven, which would indicate that God's compassion is finite (since if He were infinitely compassionate He would forgive everyone).

Therefore, we have to conclude that either the suffering of those in Hell is God's will, or God doesn't have the power to rescue every sinner. Either way we are forced to conclude that He is a flawed God.

How often will I need to use the bathroom?

As often as you like. There are no lines, the restrooms are spotless, and you never run out of cute little Labrador puppies to wipe your butt on. But don't flush them down the toilet—use the waste bins provided.

Why do bad things happen to good people?

For the same reason that good things happen to bad people: to keep everyone guessing. God has learned the hard way that delayed gratification is a much better method for motivating humans than direct conditioning or determinism, which would make us no better than monkeys trained to pull a lever to win a banana, or Calvinists.

If bad things only happened to bad people, then everyone else would be able to tell that they were "bad," and vigilante groups would assume a divine mandate to mete out their own human justice. Also, where's the incentive for a bad person to reform if nothing but bad things happen to them all the time?

You'd also end up with a self-perpetuating loop. For example, say someone covets his neighbor's ox—and then secretly seduces it. Now that's just rank and deserves divine wrath, so God gives the man bovine TB. The other villagers (let's assume for the sake of argument that he lives in a village) see the guy walking around naked, so they know what he's been up to and decide to stone him. Stoning is bad. Ergo, the villagers would be able to justify any amount of retributive violence, since the fact that God was allowing it to happen means that He must approve, and that the recipient is bad, and hence deserving of even more punishment. The logical conclusion is that even the smallest misdemeanor escalates into a vigilante death sentence.

Hence, if God only punished the bad, we would all end up under Sharia'h law.

Will we work?

If you call being nice to other people work. You store up karma by doing good deeds on earth, and then you can spend this in Heaven. Karma is the local currency, and most angels store it in their fanny packs; you'll need plenty of it to purchase anything from sanitary towels to your first cloud.

The downside of this system is that people who reach Heaven with next to no karma—because they repent their sins moments before death (and then throw heads)—find it increasingly difficult to get onto the property ladder (for example Gandhi moved straight into a ten-bedroom cumulus with a thirty-six-hole golf course while Frank Sinatra had to settle for a cardboard box and pawn his Presidential Medal of Freedom just to eat).

Fortunately, you can earn more karma in Heaven by being really nice to everyone. It is also possible to borrow karma from others and pay it back with interest. While most terrestrial banks are controlled by the Prince of Darkness and other Neocons, in Heaven they are run by Buddhists, who have so much karma they practically give it away. There is also a karmic Federal Reserve, run by Archangel Gabriel and a board of governors who are responsible for karmic policy (while its critics advocate a return to the soul standard).

Can I pimp my cloud?

When your cloud demands an extreme makeover, you may be tempted to bring in your Beanie Babies, get a giant bathroom mirror that doubles as a plasma TV, and/or display your diecast NASCAR collectibles. If so, resist the urge because you clearly only just scraped into Heaven by the skin of your few remaining teeth. There's a good reason behind the expression: "You can't take it all with you." God doesn't want a heap of redneck crap cluttering up His Kingdom. That

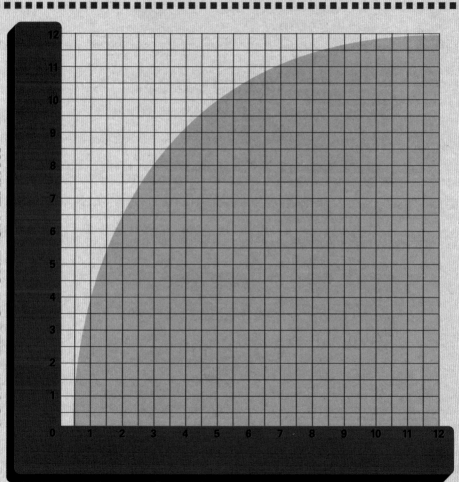

GOOD DEEDS DONE ON EARTH

KARMA PAYOUT IN HEAVEN

doesn't mean you can't freshen up that drab gray with some vibrant throws, mood lighting, and some low-maintenance potted plants. No lava lamps, Desiderata posters, or crucifixes please.

Won't Heaven be boring?

It sure used to be: everyone sitting around in the presence of God. God was more bored than anyone, because he's had more of his own company than anyone else. Then someone brought out a box of dominos, a few copies of *The National Enquirer* turned up, and someone unearthed the complete leather-bound works of Thomas Aquinas. Pretty soon God intervened, saying that things had gotten really lame, so he brought Heaven up to date, and now it offers every imaginable amenity. The karaoke bar is a big hit, and even God has been known to entertain his subjects with a few covers: "I Only Knows" (The Beach Boys), "Thank Me for the Bomb" (Ozzy Osbourne), "Dear Me" (XTC), and sometimes even "Wind Beneath My Wings" (Bette Midler) when He's really feeling good.

Do you get your own planet when you die?

The only man who has his own planet is Joseph Smith, and that's his punishment, not a reward. God intended him to teach and practice origami. But Joseph thought he said polygamy, so instead of dedicating his life to the advancement of paper engineering, he married thirty-three times and focused all his energy elsewhere.

How often do we get to see God?

Whenever you can, but don't sweat it. God understands that you will probably be so busy exploring your new surroundings that sometimes He will slip clean out of your thoughts. He doesn't mind this because He is benevolent and totally not possessive at all. He's like a parent of a toddler: He doesn't want you to hang around hugging his legs;

He wants you to explore, make friends, and have fun.

Many organized religions have lost sight of this fun approach to life. God doesn't care if people draw pictures of him, name teddy bears after his prophets, or claim that He doesn't exist. Why should He get paranoid about that when He's so perfect? God's big and bad enough to fend for himself; He doesn't need religious zealots second-guessing what He wants and intimidating others to protect his reputation. He appreciates it when humans are reverent and praise him, sure (because we all like positive feedback), but He accepts that we are only human. What really makes him happy (apart from watching girl-on-girl action) is to see us getting along peacefully with each other in Heaven and on earth.

Consider the ants: Do they fight each other or spend so much time working that they forget to enjoy life . . . oh yeah, they do actually. Okay, take the aardvark then. Now there's an animal that knows how to live large. All it needs is to stick its big nose down an anthill from time to time and it's as happy as a pig in a trough. It doesn't make bombs or bullets, or build cathedrals, but does God love the aardvark any less?

Can aardvarks stand on two legs?

Aardvarks can stand on their hind feet by resting on the base of their tail, but they can only do this for short periods of time, which makes it very difficult for them to carve stone or erect monumental Gothic structures.

THE SEVEN HEAVENLY VIRTUES

In the sixth century A.D. *when Pope Gregory defined the seven deadly sins (see page 107), he also included a corresponding set of girls' names to which we should aspire. Those who follow the Seven Heavenly Virtues—Faith, Hope, Charity, Fortitude, Justice, Prudence, and Temperance—greatly improve their chances of reaching paradise. They're all explained here, along with their respective rewards:*

Faith

Faith is belief in good things like Santa Claus, the Easter Bunny, and a benevolent monotheistic deity. Lack of Faith is belief in all the wrong things like sex before marriage, science, or that the Minnesota Vikings will ever win the Super Bowl.

In the Bible the epitome of Faith was Abraham, commanded by God to kill his son Isaac and make of him a burned offering. It's one of the most controversial scriptural stories and leaves so many questions unanswered, the foremost of which is "What in the name of holy Hell was he thinking?" Social services anyone? Exactly which bit of Abraham dancing around the campfire sharpening a big knife are Christians supposed to admire? Isaac is the one who deserves a medal, and a lifetime of therapy—lying tied up on an altar, and praying that Dad hasn't stopped taking the pills again. If God really did set Abraham a test, surely he failed spectacularly. When a divine voice commands you to barbecue your children, the sanest response is usually "I refuse to worship a sadistic supernatural being who

thinks that setting fire to minors is an appropriate form of worship" or better still, "Honey, have you seen my Risperidone? I know I left it here somewhere . . ." Only in the Old Testament could anyone get away with such epic lunacy. Try pulling an Abraham today and you'd be sectioned quicker than you can say "Jim Jones."

The reward in Heaven for those who exhibit such unquestioning Faith is eighteen months of cognitive behavioral therapy.

Hope is taking a positive future view that everything will turn out for the best and that good will triumph over evil. This isn't the same as wishful thinking, which is irrational and has no basis in fact; instead it's more like . . . religion, which teaches that everything will turn out for the best and that good will triumph over evil.

Hope

Hope is expressed by several Biblical characters, includ-ing Noah (who hoped it wouldn't rain before he'd finished varnishing the ark), Moses (who hoped no one had seen him talking to a burning bush), and the Hebrew slaves (who, after wandering in the desert for forty years, hoped that sometime soon Moses would stop and ask directions).

The Heavenly reward for those who show Hope is . . . well, Heaven.

Charity

Charity is concern for, and active helping of, others, and always carrying a lug wrench and some spare change. Put simply, it means loving thy neighbor (or thy neighbor's wife). Charity begins at home, unless you live in a gated community where you can't be door stepped by tin rattlers.

"Though I speak with the tongues of men and of angels, and have not Charity, I am become as sounding brass, or a tinkling cymbal." Yeah, but hang on, if you didn't have a tongue of men you'd become as sounding like a man without a tongue. When it comes to speaking, a tongue should always be higher up the list than Charity, along with all the other body parts that contribute to the production of articulate speech, or you may as well go home. Tongue, teeth, lips, lungs, vocal chords, soft palate, frontal and temporal lobes, Charity—in that order—otherwise you're just wasting everybody's time.

In the Bible, the Good Samaritan showed Charity when he took pity on a man who had been set upon by thieves. He went to him and bandaged his wounds, pouring on oil and wine (displaying lots of Charity but zero medical knowledge); he gave the man two silver coins, and a lug wrench, so that next time he'd be properly tooled up.

The reward in Heaven for those who have shown Charity is a lapel sticker.

Fortitude

Fortitude is never giving up, never giving in, and never saying die (even when you are actually dying). It means showing the single-mindedness of purpose to overcome every obstacle that is thrown in your path, without turning to hypnosis CDs, flaky self-help books, or religion. Ah no wait, yeah—religion's OK. You can turn to that.

In the Bible, Jeremiah, the original prophet of doom, showed remarkable Fortitude. He spent most of his life wandering naked around the streets of Jerusalem with a wooden yoke around his neck trying to warn everyone that God's judgment was at hand. No one listened, but did he give up, or take off the yoke and put on some clothes so people would take him seriously? No way. Even when he was thrown in a cistern full of mud, he kept on bumming everyone out with his dire warnings and it must have been hard work, frankly. And yet he was right all along:

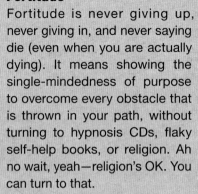
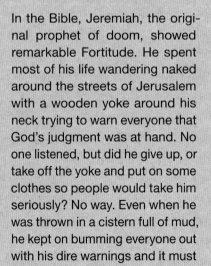

the Babylonians sacked the city, whereupon Nebuchadnezzar set him free and "Gedaliah the son of Ahikam carried him home." At this point Jeremiah must have felt pretty pissed. He had spent years looking like a complete tit and his only reward was a piggy back; no one even thought to give him a hose down. However, undeterred he carried on, seeking in vain to turn the people to the Lord. That was Jeremiah all over—as crazy as a crack addict—but at least no one could call him a quitter, although they called him lots of other things. In the end his fellow Israelites got so fed up they stoned him to death.

Reserved in Heaven for those who show Fortitude are several bags of spunk.

Justice
Justice is being fair and equitable with others, upholding what is just, fighting for what is right, fighting to do the right thing, and . . . well, basically fighting.

Sampson demonstrated this virtue. Jewish legend reliably records that his shoulders were sixty cubits broad—wider than a football field. When he wasn't wrestling Asiatic lions or washing his hair, the belligerent lug was always scrapping. He slayed one thousand Philistines with the jawbone of an ass; he set fire to the tails of three hundred foxes and the panicked beasts ran through the fields leaving lots of burning Philistines in their wake (how he actually managed to catch three hundred foxes is anybody's guess, let alone soak them in gasoline); and of course, he demolished the temple by leaning against the pillars, killing lots of . . . yes, you guessed it. Sampson sure did hate Philistines. And foxes. So there you have it: the way to Heaven is to torch wildlife and kill those who are smugly indifferent to cultural norms.

The reward for brawling against the spawn of Beelzebub is a six-figure, multi-fight contract with the UFC.

Prudence

Prudence is discretion and common sense, the ability to govern and discipline oneself by the combination of reason and sensible shoes. It's one of the trickier virtues since too much prudence can make you a real pain in the ass; the secret is balance.

King Solomon was a prudent man, the wisest and richest who ever lived, a kind of Biblical hybrid of Stephen Hawking and Bill Gates, only with contact lenses and a beard. He famously displayed his problem-solving skills when two prostitutes asked him to mediate in a custody dispute over a baby. His solution was to cut it in half, which prompted the real mother to reveal her identity by begging Solomon to offer the child to the other woman, to spare its life. And Solomon got the credit, when all along his only idea really was just to cut the baby in half. Some people get all the breaks.

Reserved in Heaven for those who show Prudence is a rubber bath mat, because you can never be too careful.

Temperance

Temperance is self-control, moderation of needed things, and abstinence from things which are not needed. It's kind of like Prudence, but you have to quit more stuff. Some people believe that Temperance involves avoiding alcohol, but they're wrong, because we all know that Temperance leads to pure distilled evil, or moonshine.

The greatest proponent of Temperance in the Bible was Jesus, when he spent forty days and nights fasting in the desert without any cigarettes. The Devil tempted him with a stone saying he could always turn it into a box of Desert Suns, but Jesus triumphed by gaining mastery over the flesh (plus God had hidden a couple of spare packets in His son's rucksack).

MEET THE PEOPLE

The first people you'll meet in Heaven are your deceased family, friends, and pets, which are a welcome and joyous sight indeed.

However, before this you will be greeted by all the amphibians that you tortured during your childhood, the animals that you ate during your time on earth, as well as every single bug that you stepped on, swatted, or sprayed. Every living entity has a right to life and killing is sinful. Therefore, it is your duty to apologize to every tiny creature that had its life curtailed prematurely by your cruelty, galumphing carelessness, and hunger. From now on you will be floating everywhere, so the chances of accidentally taking another innocent life are minimal.

After completing this admittedly lengthy process, you can finally be reunited with those you love . . . right after you've made your peace with all the vegetables.

The Bible really doesn't give us many clues about what it's like in Heaven. Why? Because "no eye has seen, nor ear heard, nor the heart of man imagined, what God has prepared for those who love Him" (1 Corinthians 2:9). In other words, our tiny human minds can't comprehend its grand splendor. That's why your reunion with loved ones—and every meal you have ever eaten—takes place in a mock-up of an Eastern European airport arrivals lounge circa 1974. No care has been spared to ease you gradually from the squalor and tedium of earthly living to the glory of Heaven. This is to prevent you from suffering sensory overload and making a spectacle of yourself (known as "jumping the cloud").

If you are a Muslim male, you will be greeted by seventy-two young virgins of "perpetual freshness"—the women of your dreams—who will lead you to palaces where you can lie on lavish thrones surrounded by gold, silver, and jewel-encrusted furnishings. All the bathrooms will have gold basins with gold taps, and as many gold tissue box covers as your heart desires. You will enjoy unlimited erotic sexual pleasures and be rewarded with the virility of a hundred men (you'll need it to fight off all the Mormons). You will also be allocated eighty thousand servants.

According to Muslim scholars, there is no Qur'anic promise of virgins for women, but at least there are no lines for the bathrooms and the hijab is optional (the Qur'an does not mandate it, and all the Imams are too busy doing virgins and beheading their servants to care).

Meet your maker

For everyone else, the most important being you will meet is, of course, God (Yahweh, Jehovah, Krishna, Buddha, Haile Selassie, L. Ron Hubbard, Flying Spaghetti Monster, etc). He/She may adopt any one of His/Her many incarnations, so don't be surprised if the Supreme One isn't immediately apparent. For example, Krishna is often depicted as a young cowherd boy playing a flute, Buddha as a recumbent smiling gentleman with a large belly, and the Christian God as a self-adhesive vinyl fish.

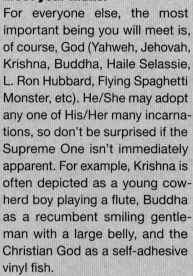

The Manifestation of the Holy Spirit is an all-consuming experience that provides total spiritual satisfaction. When you meet Him you will feel very serene, humble, and quite emotional. Whatever your opening gambit, He will have heard it all before (and will also know what you are about to say), so don't try to impress Him with witty banter. Just smile, be yourself, and engage in a little

polite worship. It isn't necessary to recite the Koran from memory or to perform your personal rendition of "Caravan of Love." Keep your veneration brief and simple, and if possible avoid anything that requires a guitar. If inspiration escapes you, anoint His feet. He loves that.

In the presence of the Holy Spirit, you may feel the urge to start shaking uncontrollably and fall backward in a trance. However, you are respectfully requested to avoid conspicuous displays of transcendent awareness. It is generally acknowledged that the best way to enjoy Heaven is in a conscious state, and you will miss much of what it has to offer if you insist on flapping around in a semi-coma talking gibberish. Plus everyone else will think you're a nutcase.

Do agnostics get into Heaven?

God cares about how many times His flock attends church/mosque/synagogue, how many candles they light, the length of their beards, and how many refrigerators they own. For sure. But above all, He rewards those who have led a good life in accordance with their consciences and He even forgives some of those who haven't.

Belief in a Universal Creator is no longer a prerequisite for admittance to the Heavenly Kingdom, but don't mention your agnosticism, as it can be a touchy subject with those who have clocked up thousands of hours of religious observance on earth. If you have spent a lifetime of eremitic austerity to attain Heavenly riches, it can be quite galling at the Pearly Gates to come face to face with Albert Camus, Kurt Cobain, and a herd of okapi.

God is quite laidback about the whole business of belief and takes every opportunity to mess with people's heads (otherwise known as "working in mysterious ways"). He let Bertrand Russell and Adolf Eichmann into Heaven,

and delights in recounting the time when the nihilistic, old racist Friedrich Nietzsche arrived and blushingly blurted out, "God, I thought you were dead!" If Osama bin Laden ever makes it into Paradise, you can be sure that every one of his seventy-two virgins will be men. That's one of the first things you'll notice about God (apart from his nose hair): He's got an awesome sense of humor and loves to play practical jokes.

Heaven is full of contradictions. For instance, God has limitless patience and His love for you is unconditional, but he'll throw an Old Testament fit if you dare ask if He created everything, who created Him? He will no doubt tersely explain that He is outside of the human construct of time and therefore not subject to the law of cause and effect. Or He might simply change the subject by asking you to guess how many fingers He's holding up behind His back. Don't push your luck. Angels have been kicked out of Heaven

for less. Satan fell from grace for questioning why round pizzas are delivered in square boxes, and for insisting that boysenberry is one of the twenty-three flavors of Dr. Pepper (he was right, but he still got smacked because God can't stand smartasses).

Celebrity angels

You will see lots of famous faces here, from Steve Fossett (in case you were wondering) to Genghis Khan (who has apologized for killing twenty million people and now coaches the Little League team), and there are heaps of movie stars and sporting legends. While a select few are happy to sign autographs and have a quick chat, most will tell you to go to Hell (no one said you need a sense of irony to get into Heaven). And who can blame them: Imagine spending earthly life as a privileged celebrity, only to find that everyone has the same benefits in Heaven as you had on earth, only they are blessed with anonymity, while you get constantly harassed by people like you.

The most miserable people in heaven are, of course, the gurus and prophets, such as John the Baptist, Elijah, and that Swami with all the Rolls Royces whom the Beatles visited during the sixties. No one is interested in the opening act once the headliner enters the stadium.

The twenty-five people you meet in Heaven

Inevitably there are far more annoying people in Heaven than there are in Hell, and you may often catch yourself asking under your breath, "How on earth did they get in here?"

Hell doesn't have the monopoly on people who really get on your nerves. You'll just have to learn to tolerate them, because you can only achieve Heaven on earth by exercising tolerance, love, peace, and understanding. Why should it be any different in Heaven? So grit your teeth and welcome with open arms the many opportunities for patience and open-mindedness

that will come your way every day. Here are twenty-five types of people that will help you to develop forbearance; people who:

1. Crack their knuckles and drum on every available surface.

2. Walk slowly in front of you in groups.

3. Deny your right to hate them.

4. Ask for sleeves for cold drinks in Starbucks, like their iced caramel latte is too hot to hold.

5. Ask for their drinks to be extra hot.

6. Ask if they can "borrow" something when they really mean "have," like a piece of paper or one of your cigarettes.

7. Post a few nude pictures on their blogs and then suddenly stop.

8. Comment on what you are eating.

9. Point at their wrist when asking for the time.

10. Make a stupid face when they don't understand something, and who consequently spend the whole time making a stupid face.

11. Can bend their thumb so that it touches their wrist.

12. Eat potato chips loudly in a variety of situations.

13. Fill their ice trays as soon as they become empty.

14. Upload your video to YouTube and then get more views than your better quality version.

15. Have dimples on their knees.

16. Think that the way they tie the laces on their sneakers automatically makes them way cooler than you.

17. Search for the face of Jesus or Mohammed in the vegetable section of a supermarket.

18. Warn you of the dangers of staring directly at a total solar eclipse.

19. Move into another country and then try to change its religion.

20. Post nothing but song lyrics on their blogs.

21. Say "It'll happen when you least expect it!"

22. Say "vuh" instead of "the."

23. Try to fuse Western cartoons with anime.

24. Never have cravings.

25. Use the word "fabulous" to describe curtains.

ETIQUETTE

Etiquette is a topic that has occupied writers and thinkers in all sophisticated societies for millennia. In Heaven you will find most people are nicer to you if you behave politely and show respect to the social norms. However, you'll generally discover that everyone is fairly laidback, since all the uptight people are so busy going to the gym or having colonics that you rarely see them out in public. The sign above the Pearly Gates gives you the first hint that the atmosphere is relaxed: NO SHOES, NO SHIRT, NO WORRIES.

Meeting and greeting

The customary greeting is to raise your arms in an open gesture of acceptance. Many point their index finger and adopt a languid, casual pose (see Raphael's painting called "The Three Graces"). Others touch their halos as a sign of respect. You may hug, kiss, or shake hands (limply—no need to prove anything now). Because this is Heaven, whatever greeting you choose will be in perfect synch with the other person. Wondering how many cheeks to kiss or whether to back slap are earthly concerns. Anything goes as long as you smile and maintain good eye contact (especially if the other person isn't wearing any clothes).

Personal space is large. Maintain at least a wing's length of distance between you and someone else, as it can be tricky to close the gap without poking someone in the face or breaking a limb. The answer to the question, "How many angels can dance on

53

the head of a pin?" is "No more than three at a time, in order to minimize soft-tissue injuries." It has been said that an angel's wing could easily break a man's arm but such incidents are rare. Angels aren't naturally violent creatures, unless you blatantly mess with them. However, folks here don't always turn the other cheek, and when provoked an angel will think nothing of jabbing you where it counts with a feathery appendage.

Body language

Always say hello to everyone. Maintain good posture. Slouching is not encouraged. Don't use the thumbs-up sign: It means "this is my thumb" and is unlikely to win you any awards for conversation openers.

Littering will not be tolerated. If you drop so much as a candy wrapper you are likely to be told off by another angel. Heaven, like Switzerland, is clean and litter-free; please try to keep it that way.

Even though there are no cars in Heaven, there are traffic lights and jaywalking is highly discouraged. Always wait for the FLOAT/DON'T FLOAT sign to turn green before crossing.

Dress

You will arrive in Heaven in the clothes you were wearing when you departed from earth. If you died in your sleep commando-style, this is nothing to be embarrassed about. Nakedness is as natural as it was in the Garden of Eden before the arrival of original sin. However, that won't stop people pointing at you and having a good laugh at your expense.

Most people change into an all-purpose white shift, since temperature and fashion aren't issues here. Ease of movement is important, since you won't want anything restricting you as you flit gracefully from cloud to cloud. Fashionable clothing is generally avoided, since it is considered divisive and all body types are equally valid, even the fat ugly ones. Footwear is also optional. Sandals are commonplace, while German angels favor Birkenstocks (old habits die hard).

Conversation

In Heaven, the expression "any friend of yours is a friend of yours" is a good description of the social scene. Initially, angels can seem quite formal, though polite, and a bit preoccupied, but they relax after you become more familiar to them. The status quo prevails, so making new friends is not a major priority. Everyone is rather honest and straightforward, if a tad conservative. Respect the privacy of others and do not ask personal questions about how people died or their earthly politics, income, or religious beliefs.

If you're stuck for conversation, it is acceptable to hum a Gregorian chant quietly to yourself until inspiration strikes (or until someone tells you to stop it). Discussing laundry detergent is popular, since even immortal beings are prone to stubborn stains and are always looking for ways to minimize their ironing.

Angels are very well behaved, and sticklers for doing things the right way the first time. They also obey the rules by the book. They'll take you literally (irony is not understood), so idle promises or invitations such as "we must do this again sometime" will be taken at face value. They are also excellent listeners. If someone is talking, don't interrupt. Always wait until the other angel has finished speaking (or nodding silently).

Don't keep smiling, making jokes, or being over-friendly too soon. You will gain more trust and respect if you are restrained and dignified at first. Friendship is built slowly (why rush when you've got all eternity?); over-familiarity is considered superficial and viewed with distrust. Angels don't smile much—not because they are miserable, but because they like to keep their emotions under control. If you are feeling happy, you may allow a slight enigmatic upturn of the lips. If you are feeling sad, take some antidepressants and stay in bed for the day. Anger is rarely expressed directly; it might be vented with a smirk or by someone flipping you the bird behind your back.

In Heaven, brownnosing lubricates the wheels of social interaction. You should aim to include at least five compliments in every sentence. If you find this distracting, then before you start a conversation it is permissible to present a short letter or Powerpoint demonstration to express sincere gratitude for the existence of the assembled company and which succinctly lists all the reasons why you admire them for their flair, vision, outstanding talent, remarkable selflessness, etc. (People from California usually find that this comes naturally.)

Table manners

Cut food with your knife and use your utensils or hands to bring it to your mouth. Keep it simple: chew, swallow, and move on. Anything else is window-dressing, though it's customary to laugh heartily whenever Jesus pokes bread sticks through the two holes in his palms. He finds it super funny, even though nobody else does.

The custom with regard to how much food to leave on your plate at the end of the meal differs between cultures. In Eastern culture, it is traditional to leave some food on your plate, to imply that you are satisfied. In Western culture, it is customary to clear your plate to demonstrate that you are in the advanced stages of coronary heart disease.

ACCOMMODATIONS

Heaven offers a peaceful, honest, and sharing environment, but with its high standard of living and population density, real estate is at a premium: think Monaco minus the casinos and the French.

The central area of Heaven is not huge, and a fit person can float quite comfortably between attractions. However, it can be very tiring trekking around the clouds and too much reliance on hot air currents might fray your temper. It's worth taking some time to consider what would be the best area in which to stay. Do you want to be near transport for daytrips outside Heaven (to attend a séance or visit relatives) or do you want to wander back to your hotel along tiny medieval streets paved with recycled household waste?

You'll undoubtedly have a great time, wherever you choose to stay, but hotel location is bound to make a difference to your celestial experience. However, it is vital that you follow a few simple rules, otherwise communal living on this scale inevitably breaks down. When everyone sings from the same hymn sheet, they can be as happy as the proverbial clam (despite the fact that edible bivalve mollusks are conspicuous by their absence in all references to Utopia, both scriptural and secular). Hence, you should keep communal areas clean and tidy, do not prop open or obstruct any fire doors, and avoid playing the harp or singing God's praises between 11 p.m. and 7 a.m. In cases of noise disturbance, normally one verbal or written warning will be given. Thereafter, you will be cast into

Purgatory for a thousand years, where a man who looks suspiciously like Johnny Knoxville will kick you repeatedly in the groin (if you are a woman you will be sent to Saudi Arabia).

Apart from clouds, the establishment you choose for your time in Heaven will fulfill your every whim, and more than compensate for the mediocre service and surroundings that you have come to accept on earth. Here is a sample of the privileged 1,374,561 hotels in Heaven that are given a "Hotels to Die For" rating. Our choice selection is synonymous with quality and tradition, as well as fulfilling your wildest fantasies.

Mussolini's

This Renaissance-style property sits on one thousand manicured lakeside acres and sets the standard by which every other hotel in Heaven is measured. It offers a veritable feast for the senses: hand-painted ceilings, Venetian chandeliers, and fifteenth century Flemish tapestries—and that's just the closets. In the restrooms, every sheet of toilet paper has been hand-painted by Sandro Botticelli using true linear perspective, the urinals are sculpted in shallow relief style by Donatello, and the marbling on the hand dryers is so exquisite one would never guess it was faux. We'll leave a description of the actual rooms to your wildest dreams; even then they will be surpassed.

The hotel represents a delicate balance of refinement and luxury, and it has welcomed the most high-profile and illustrious clientele—but don't let the ornate surroundings put you on your best behavior. Relax and enjoy this home away from home. You can eat your dinner in your sweats and no one will bat an eyelash. You can scratch your ass in the lobby in full sight of the hotel's most distinguished guests, or fart triumphantly in the crowded lift, and your conduct will be deemed the epitome of sophistication. You dictate the etiquette and everyone else will fall into line. Whether you are looking to have a quiet weekend break or invade Abyssinia, you can be assured that this place will cater to your every need.

New Jerusalem

Revelation 21:2-3 tells us we will have a new home called "New Jerusalem" which means "city of peace." It should more accurately be described as a giant hotel complex 1,500 miles wide, 1,500 miles long, and 1,500 miles high, accessible through any one of its 1,200 gates, each of which bears the name of an Israeli splinter group.

The entire hotel is constructed of gold and jewels—even the foundations are made of precious stones. It offers the highest level of service found anywhere in Heaven and God's glory shines through the walls to produce a breathtaking rainbow of colors. As you would expect from an establishment of this caliber, many of the suites have open fireplaces and decked balconies, a 42-inch HD-ready plasma TV, and high-speed wireless broadband access. On arrival, each guest receives a complimentary welcome buffet with a choice of teas, fresh coffee, communion wafers, and handmade matza balls.

The Spawny Upgradia

You know how every time you stay in a hotel there's always someone who gets double booked and receives a complimentary stay in the bridal suite as a result? Or the couple in front of you checking in announces they just got married and get a free crate of bubbly? Well this time it's your turn to get preferential treatment. Every day is your birthday, honeymoon, and a you're-the-millionth-customer promotion. So when you go down to the self-service breakfast, you won't have to meekly let the nice old lady in front of you take the last fried egg and triangle of fried bread, because they have little cocktail flags sticking out of them that say RESERVED. You'll get the last booking at the squash court, and in the evening it's you who empties the gaming machine in the hotel bar with your first coin. They'll be so many freebies coming your way that guest-envy will soon become a distant memory.

Bukkake Plaza

This is just like those Japanese love hotels back on earth, only there the rooms are filled with sad commuters committing adultery. The Bukkake Plaza offers horny little angels the opportunity to get all excited over their ideal fantasy partners, with no strings attached. A wall of video monitors shows which rooms are available. Simply input the details and characteristics of your perfect lover and they will be lying passively on the oversized bed when you enter your room. You can even request real people who are still alive. Simply type in "Brad" or "Angelina" (or "Brangelina" if you fancy a threesome), "Britney" or "Justin," "Barack" or "Hillary"

(you kinky old devil) and they will be beamed up during their sleep. Upon waking they will think they've had a vivid dream, and no harm done. Who said Heaven can't be this much fun?

Waffles

On first appearance, Waffles seems to belie its multi-star rating because it doesn't have a single restaurant or even room service. So what is the secret of its unprecedented popularity?

Everything in the hotel is edible, from the doorknobs to the curtain poles, the fax machines to the RECYCLE YOUR TOWELS sign. If you wake in the middle of the night and fancy a snack, simply break a piece off the headboard or take a bite out of your pillow, and if you get the taste for something more substantial, the charming bell hop, Bernd Jürgen Brandes, is happy to oblige.

The attention to detail here is unsurpassed. We recommend you don't leave without sampling the curtains, the trouser press, and the botanical drawings above the bed. Every feature in the room has been designed to surprise and delight. For starters, pick the matted hair out of the bath plug and enjoy an intriguing blend of bird's nest and gazpacho soup; for your main course, flush the toilet, and when the handle breaks off in your hand, pop it in your mouth and a full turkey dinner will explode on the back of your tongue; finally, lick the wall behind the toilet and you'll be rewarded with a lemon cheesecake taste sensation. The battery case of the TV remote may be taped in place, but peel it off, bite down and . . . oh no, wait a minute, that is just tape, but rest assured that everything else is up for grabs. After you've stayed here you won't want to eat anywhere else.

Hotel Slalom

This fantastic winter-themed entertainment destination is set in some of the best Alpine-style mountains in Heaven. It offers myriad activities throughout the year to suit the most demanding tastes. One of the goals of the Slalom Resort is to ensure that no one gets cold or is made to feel stupid. With this in mind, the climate maintains a constant ambient temperature and the skiing is all uphill. Not only is this much safer, it eliminates the need for ski lifts, which spoil the view and are scary as Hell anyway. When you reach the top of the mountain, discard your disposable skis and simply walk down again.

Everyone usually sports regulation short, wide, waxless skis, and Slalom's year-round winter theme is made possible due to a virtual ski surface technology called Rubbersnow, which never melts, and bounces you back on your feet whenever you fall over. If anyone laughs at your ineptitude, simply smile and tell them to go to Hell.

Hollywood Hotel

Ever fantasized of re-enacting a scene from one of your favorite movies? Well now is your chance. Simply place a request at reception and the attentive staff will have one of its three sound studios ready to roll before the porter has even had time to take your luggage. Perhaps you dream of being James Dean in *East of Eden*: "She ain't no good and I ain't no good. I knew there was a reason why I wasn't . . . I hate her and I hate him, too." Or how about the suburban housewife in *Brief Encounter*: "I want to die; if only I could die . . ." or, Heaven's most popular request, John Belushi in *Animal House:* "Hey! What's this lying around shit?" There are so many memorable scenes to explore, so many dearly departed actors to help you realize the dream.

RESTAURANTS AND EATERIES

Heaven is blessed with an abundant landscape which is permanently bathed in the eternal sunshine of God's light. Everywhere your senses will be assaulted by the sight and smells of lush vegetation, rolling green hills, and verdant pastures, all irrigated and nourished by the sweet and cooling waters of the River of Life. Behold the paradise where God's chosen flock grazes for eternity.

As the breathtaking beauty of this magnificent vista slowly sinks in, you could be forgiven for thinking that eating here is heavily biased in favor of God's flock. And you'd be right: There is no escaping the fact that grass is the staple diet in Heaven, but if you know where to look, there is a plethora of modern and ethnically complex alternatives for those with an adventurous spirit or a single stomach.

There is a wide spectrum of cellulose-free dining to suit every palette. Eating establishments range from dusty roadside stalls where sharply-dressed street hawkers with perfect teeth offer brightly-colored deep-fried delicacies smothered in peanut sauce, to smart air-conditioned restaurants where snooty servers bring you microscopic portions of food that nevertheless leave you feeling totally satisfied.

We've compiled this short list of some of the most popular venues to help you navigate the bewildering array of specialities:

Salome's

If you want food that resonates simplicity and singleness of vision, look no further than Salome's, the brainchild of Old Testament prophet and decapitated doyenne of degustation, John the Baptist. Before setting up his eaterie, John was a true man of purpose from the pages of Scripture, and the menu expresses his renunciation of worldly pursuits. The service is slick yet unobtrusive, and the muted lighting and camel-hair furnishings effortlessly create just the right mood of self-mortification.

The kitchen delivers no-nonsense ascetic food in dignified, historic surroundings. When did you last have locusts and wild honey on the same plate? Whether you opt for the homemade locust and honey sausage, or the char-grilled locust rump steak with peppered honey sauce, or even the hot compote of locust, you can guarantee that the insect base notes in every dish will be perfectly complimented by the sweetness of the honey. Heading the puddings is the locust crème brûlée, or if you want comfort food, why not try the splendid locust and honey crumble?

John's philosophy can best be summed up by the maxim: "I just love eating locusts. They're yummy."

The Hidden Manna

In a tabernacle tucked away behind a large cloudy pillar, this cozy kosher café owes much to owner Moses' and wife Zipporah's enthusiasm for functional desert-survival fare. This homely spot boasts a blend of old and new world, furnished with a mélange of antique camping furniture and military memorabilia, where the couple have realized their vision of a "forty-years-in-the-wilderness" style restaurant widely considered to be one of the best eateries in Heaven. While the choice of food is somewhat limited, son Gershom collects the manna fresh every day and is constantly dreaming up new ways to cook and serve this chewy, bland, and unappetizing pulp. How anyone could live on this mush for a week, let alone four decades, is unfathomable, but this Hasidic hideaway is perennially popular with a broad spread of the Jewish diaspora, from hardcore Zionists to Mossad hitmen.

While the menu offers traditional fare, the cocktails cater to Jews and gentiles alike: Israeli classics such as the world-famous Gaza Wallbanger (2 oz. vodka, 4 oz. fresh orange juice, 1 large bulldozer) rub shoulders with an impressive choice of pork and shellfish milkshakes.

TKs

TKs remains one of the best places to grab a light bite and experience the guilty thrill of original sin. The food speaks for itself: pluck a talking apple from the large gnarly Tree of Life that forms the centerpiece of this historic venue and bask in the shade of its ancient boughs as you contemplate man's fall from his state of innocence. After the fruit has finished explaining the theory of special relativity, or answered some of your fundamental philosophical questions about knowledge and reality, such as why they put braille dots on the keypad of drive-through ATMs, sink your teeth into its succulent flesh. The flavors are complex and intense—somewhere between a late-season Braeburn and Appletize. Fig leaves are provided for any customers who have forgotten to bring their underwear.

Foresight

The only revolving roof top restaurant in Heaven owes its creation

67

to proprietor Prophet Ezekiel's unique vision. In the opening chapter of the Old Testament Book of Ezekiel, which to some up here has become something of a foodie Bible, he describes where he got his inspiration:

And it came to pass in the thirtieth year, in the fourth month, in the fifth day of the month as I was among the captives by the river of Chebar, that I saw visions of God. I looked, and, behold, a whirlwind came from the north and out of the midst thereof came four living creatures and a large wheel covered with eyes. And every one had four faces, and four wings. And the sole of a calf's feet and they all sparkled like burnished brass. And when I saw it, I fell upon the ground and nearly crapped myself. As for the likeness of their faces, they were of a man, lion, ox, and an eagle. But as I stood there trying not to soil my robe I beheld a business opportunity and figureth that if I could open a revolving rooftop restaurant that would tar-

get this consumer base, it would be liken to having four times the number of punters, and I could make a big wedge of mullah. Verily it had all the appearance of a no-brainer.

His signature dish is of course, Ezekiel Stew, a recipe handed down from none other than the Divine Architect himself, who reveals how to make it in Ezekiel 24 (Take a look for yourself. Really, you couldn't make this stuff up.)

The Hall of the Slain

The Vikings believed that after death a great warrior would be swept away by female warriors called Valkyries to live in Valhalla, a giant pub also known as the "Hall of the Slain" which was run by Odin, the king of the gods. Here they would wait until judgment day at the end of time, when an epic fight would kick off in the giant parking lot outside just after Final Closing Time. It would be fought between the gods (the forces of good) and the giants (tall

HALL OF
THE SLAIN!!!

people). The souls of the dead warriors would fight on the side of the gods.

The Hall offers a three-course meal for less than ten dollars, and there is a playground in the beer garden. It is advisable to book ahead for parties of more than eight hundred.

Sodom

Rumor has it that after perishing in the fire and brimstone of Sodom and Gomorrah, God relented and allowed its doomed inhabitants into Heaven after realizing that their love of "going after strange flesh" was a reference to their passion for exotic meats. Some of them carried on the tradition by clubbing together and opening this French-Jordanian fusion restaurant with nothing more than a few coins in their pockets, heads filled with dreams, and a wheelbarrow filled with salt. Today this thriving hub offers classic bistro dishes; expect to find frogs' legs and hummus salad, moules marinières, and a wide selection of freshly made soups.

Taco Libre

This fast-food chain offers authentic Tex-Mex cuisine, without the bowel complications or congestive heart failure: incredible guacamole, fresh salsa, piping hot tortillas, and Lone Star and iced margaritas on tap. The chihuahua chalupas are so big that if you weren't already dead you'd pop an artery trying to finish them. There can be no greater endorsement than the sight of real Mexicans eating here: Emiliano Zapata and Pancho Villa can be spotted most days discussing revolutionary politics over a plate of cheesaritos.

The Loaves and Fishes

Jesus made his name with his signature miracle: the feeding of five thousand people. Al fresco seafood dining doesn't come any better than this, especially when you find yourself on a hill overlooking a lake, it's getting late, and you can't be bothered to cook.

The menu has evolved considerably since biblical times, and now offers grilled sea bass, Maryland crab cakes with a chili-spiked aioli, and lobster thermidor served in a sesame bun with a miso-flavored mayonnaise. The portion sizes are small, but if you are still hungry at the end of the meal there are always several baskets of scraps left over.

The Fatted Calf

Part of a restaurant franchise which includes the Lost Sheep and the Lost Coin, the Fatted Calf is the ideal venue to celebrate a reunion. Boasting the smallest selection of humble pie outside of the White House, it attracts a young crowd of freeloading prodigals who have splurged their inheritance on rich food and loose women, and are now looking to fleece some more cash from their gullible and overindulgent fathers. It's the ideal place to encourage sibling rivalry or to simply soak up the atmosphere of seething jealousy and righteous indignation.

The Last Supper Club

The Last Supper Club's private room can accommodate groups of up to thirteen. Its staff can help to plan your brunch or farewell party, or any event where a group of people come together to share bread and wine in a sophisticated atmosphere of transubstantiation for Catholics or extended metaphor for all other religions. Napkins are provided for customers whose cups runneth over.

B12

Many world religions view vegetarianism as the ideal diet for spiritual progress: Gnostics were primarily vegetarians along with many present-day Hindus, Jains, and Buddhist monks. However, this trendy bistro mainly caters to smug hippies and feminist lefties, so that the rest of us don't have our evenings ruined by their people-hating antics (and body odor).

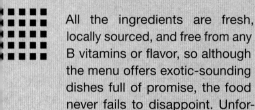

All the ingredients are fresh, locally sourced, and free from any B vitamins or flavor, so although the menu offers exotic-sounding dishes full of promise, the food never fails to disappoint. Unfortunately, even in Heaven veggie food really isn't that appealing. Whether you opt for the goat's cheese risotto, raw nori rolls, or the quinoa and bulgur wheat tabouli, you'll still need to eat a kebab on the way home if you want to avoid chronic anemia.

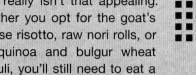

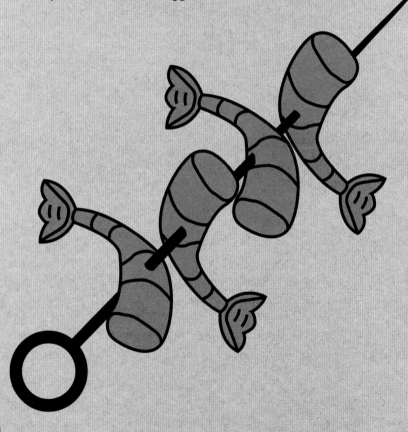

SHOPPING

Whoever says money can't buy happiness simply doesn't know where to shop. On earth, shopping is about as much fun as opening a banana crate and finding a Brazilian spider, whereas in Heaven it's an absolute scream (although screaming is discouraged, so it's more like a sanctimonious squeal).

Even if you hate shopping more than seeing Richard Simmons in spandex, you will quickly discover that it can be very enjoyable when all the factors that you normally associate with it have been removed. Endless lines, sociopathic sales staff, pestering children, artificial sale prices, air-conditioning that sucks all the moisture out of the top of your head as soon as you cross the threshold leaving you convuls-ing in the doorway gagging for a saline drip—you name an irritation, major or minor, and Heaven will sweep it away to ensure that nothing hampers your retailing pleasure.

Just a block west of God's Throne of Glory is the exclusive Wings and Holy Things Mart, where you can buy anything from a new halo to bars of rubber soap (very popular with nuns and ex-cons-turned-do-gooders). The center is within easy walking distance of the main gate of Heaven, so you can start shopping as soon as you arrive. This is where the rich and famous pick up their knickknacks. The dead celebs are easy to spot, since they still insist on drawing attention to themselves by their ludicrous attempts at anonymity: sunglasses the size of satellite dishes, $1,720 Louis Vuitton eco-friendly "Love" satchels, purses bigger than their egos, heels so steep they have to balance on one toe, etc.

The Mart has an unrivalled selection of quality shops that offer a traditional alternative to the mega malls, those huge oppressive kingdoms of gleaming glass and steel with tiled fountains and highly polished halls stretching to the horizon. In Heaven, we get back to basics, to the ethos of the corner shops and community stores which have all but died out, slowly choked by the likes of Wal-Mart, Kmart, Target, and Kroger.

Visit the old-style grocery store on Church Street, where a kind man with a moustache will ruffle your hair and give you a Garibaldi biscuit from a glass-topped tin. Two doors down there's a gentleman's outfitters, where you'll be covered from head to toe with white chalk and then sexually assaulted on the flimsy pretext of being "measured up." The sparsely-stocked toy shop offers a limited choice

of wooden toys: spinning tops in red or blue, a puppet theater, and assorted pieces of two-by-four spruce lumber (for stickball, of course, although you'll have to use a lump of coal or your father's recently-removed gall bladder for the ball).

Shopping should be about luxuries and fulfilling fantasies, not trudging around buying staple goods. In Heaven, the only limit is your own imagination. Here's a list of some of the best shopping locales—grab your celestial shopping cart and prepare to shop until you drop! (And even that'll be okay since you'll already be in Heaven anyway.)

The Body Shop

You've got a big date coming up and you need a special something to make you feel pampered and super sexy. Why waste time and money on skincare products to keep body and soul together when you can pick up a perfect new bod? Bag a sassy chassis

BODY SHOP

(available in sizes eight to sixteen) and everyone will want a piece of your natty anatomy. Try it on for size, give it a test drive, and if you are anything less than totally satisfied, return it in tip-top condition (take a shower, exfoliate, and refrain from sex for twenty-four hours) and keep browsing until you find a physical structure that's hotter than a six-peckered alley cat. And there's no danger of turning up to a party looking the same as anyone else, because all the products are unique, down to the very last fingerprint. (See also Fingerhut.)

Wings-R-Us

The ultimate emporium of feather-covered modified forelimbs, this airy store has the biggest selection of flight-aids this side of Jacob's Ladder. From majestic obsidian behemoths to carbon fiber mono-sails, and from helicopter rotor blades to buffalo wings, there are pinions by the millions to suit all tastes. Free feathery halo and deluxe glitter wand with every purchase.

GAP

True to its name, this store doesn't sell clothes; it sells gaps. The moment you enter the large recently-refurbished showroom you'll be confronted by the whole kit and caboodle: cracks and crannies, slits and gullies of all shapes and sizes coming at you, from tooth cavities to canyons. Normally you'd expect gaps to be the ultimate niche market, and you probably think you need a hole like you need a hole in the head, but you'd be surprised how indispensable they can be, especially when performing miracles. Whether you want stigmata, to part the Red Sea, or make a small room appear bigger, GAP offers the whole enchilada without burning a hole in your pocket! And if you want to raze the walls of Jericho, you won't need seven priests blowing ram's horns. Just apply a wall-sized gap and hey presto: a fissure that's big enough to drive a truck through.

Goodcock Home Furniture & More

Premium furnishings that are guaranteed to give you wood, at affordable prices. Established in 2005 by lifelong bachelor and suave balladeer-turned-upholsterer, Luther Vandross, Goodcock Home Furniture & More offers a full range of furniture and bedding, underscored by Luther's extraordinary soft furnishing skills. Never before has homeware offered such a thrilling aphrodisiac for the senses. There's no place to hide, so don't run from what you feel, because a house is not a home unless there's chairs to call your own. Its slogan says it all: "Goodcock will treat you right, we'll have a sweet time, baby, all night. Mmmm, yeah, you are my shining star, doo doo doo doo, etc."

Mary's Secret

The scene, the style, and not a pair of lace-on-lace Brazilian-cut panties in sight. Hip huggers, cheekies, and thongs are a thing of the past. Say "Hasta la vista" to Diamanté halter babydolls, "screw you" to Peek-a-boo, and tell G-strings to get knotted; there's no longer any need to get strung out by cheese wire up your fanny. All the lingerie in this sensible and modestly-priced boutique was inspired by asking one simple question: "WWMW?" or "What would Madonna wear?" (Not her; the other one.) The answer came back with a resounding, unequivocal commitment to good old-fashioned comfort over style: elephantine granny knickers with elastic waistbands that cover your belly button, quilted flannelette dressing gowns, and tights that are so thick you can use them to felt roofs. There is no actual mention in the Bible that the Blessed Virgin wore any of this stuff, so in keeping with religious scholarly tradition, we made something up. Hurry down while stockings last!

Advertisements

TV and billboard advertising is heavily regulated because you don't need a bunch of overpaid creatives undermining your self-esteem and telling you you're worthless. That's what your family is for.

Better still, ads in Heaven can't play on human insecurities by claiming products will improve our lives and bring us happiness because everything is already perfect. So ads here are a pleasure to watch because they are honest, straightforward, and tell you what you need to know. If they say "the taste of real . . . ," "studies have shown . . . ," and "for a limited time only" then it has to be God's honest truth.

Some examples:
1. All grocery ads feature meals doing what they do best—sitting quietly on a plate waiting to be eaten. At no time will you be subjected to food that talks, sings, or dances.

2. Jingles are required to be atonal and totally unmemorable so that there is no chance of one of them looping endlessly in your head so you have to force a screwdriver up your nose to make it stop.

3. Pensions and life insurance ads can't exploit your fear of ending your life penniless smelling of stale urine, or taking a dirt nap without providing for your family, because you're already dead.

4. BANNED: Espresso makers that only work with specially designed "pods" that are meant to brew the perfect cup of coffee with the minimum of fuss and the maximum of style.

5. Skin-care creams won't make totally absurd claims like "Wrinkles hate it!" (Since when did wrinkles become sentient beings?) or, "Our product challenges the signs of aging!" (That's definitely not the same as getting rid of them, pal).

6. Never again will you have to sit through a commercial in which a Z-list celebrity squirms painfully on a heavily-discounted sofa, trying to look like she's relaxing in the height of luxury and refined comfort.

7. "Terms and Conditions apply" (in small letters). Everything you've just wasted the last thirty seconds watching is complete baloney. In Heaven, this kind of blatant lying is punishable by stoning.

8. Beer ads don't blather on about leaving the hops to brew longer for a fuller flavor. They tell it how it is—"Carlsberg Special Brew: It makes you talk in another language, then fall over. Probably the best lager in the world for putting you on the transplant list. Actually, we haven't a clue why we pay millions of bucks for prime time slots because our demographic doesn't have a TV, or a job, or a house, or any friends for that matter. Our demographic is sitting on a park bench shouting at squirrels in that weird gutteral voice, the lingua-franca of winos the world over."

9. BANNED: disposable razors with more than one blade. How is it that as a society we have come to accept that only razors that offer a minimum of at least six blades are up to the job of removing a little facial hair? This is a great illustration of how manufacturers gradually reduce the quality and effectiveness of their products so that we soon have to pay more for a so-called premium product to gain the equivalent performance of an entry-level item fifty years ago.

ENTERTAINMENT

Believe it or not, your free time in Heaven won't be completely taken up by choir rehearsals or practicing the harp. Oh, holy heck, no! Times have really changed, so you can expect to have plenty of fun, and even soak up a little culture in the process.

Remember, many of the great artists, writers, composers, performers, filmmakers, actors, and musicians are now in Heaven, so every day there's a packed schedule of entertainment that will appeal to a wide range of tastes. Take your pick: Attend an original symphony from the quills of the classical greats, watch Rubens (the most prolific painter the world has ever known) unveil yet another study of female cellulite, or take a try at Leonardo da Vinci's most recently invented gaming console.

And if you can't be bothered to leave your cloud or hotel room, then you can choose from thousands of cable channels, showing programs new and old, everything from *Queer Eye for the Straight Sprite* to endless reruns of *Mr. Dead.* Here are some listings for fun activities that are happening near you:

Movies

Please note that all movies in Heaven are subject to fairly strict censorship. While God is a strong advocate of free expression, you may find that some of your favorite flicks have been subtly edited to make them more appropriate for celestial viewing. God doesn't do it; he doesn't have to, when there is an army of sanctimonious self-appointed cinema sanitizers falling over themselves to make movies "safe" for families by editing out sex, violence, and foul language. At times, they even rewrite endings that aren't entirely happy.

Silence of the Lambs: A brilliant psychiatrist and cannibalistic serial killer becomes a Quaker and discovers the pleasures of vegetarian cooking.

Kiss Bill Vol. 1 and 2: An epic-length domestic drama with homages to earlier genres, such as *The Waltons* and *Little House on the Prairie*. At the beginning of the movie Beatrix "Black Mamba" Potter tells Bill that she is pregnant with his child. They get married and buy a saw mill in the Blue Ridge Mountains where he teaches tai chi while she writes and illustrates children's books.

Ichi the Killer: When a Yakuza boss named Anjo disappears with three hundred million yen, his chief henchman, a sadomasochistic man named Kakihari and the rest of his goons chalk it up to experience and turn the other cheek.

The Deer Hunter: After a wedding scene lasting less than two minutes, a trio of steelworkers from Pennsylvania become hippies and bring an end the Vietnam War through peaceful protest.

Saw: The Cut Edition: Two men find themselves locked in a disused bathroom with instructions for one to kill the other, or he and his family will be killed. They spend two hours in silent prayer, until the police arrive and set them free. Game over.

Opera
To paraphrase Mark Twain: "I hate opera worse than having a chilli enema." Fine sentiments indeed, but in Heaven opera is less elitist, shorter, and much less camp. No performers are allowed to express emotion by repeatedly putting their clenched fists in front of their faces and sing-laughing ("A-ha-ha-ha-ha-ha") is forbidden, as well as sing-crying ("A-ha-ha-ha-ha-ha"). Also, the plot is always spoken in English. The audience wave big foam hands, you can buy

83

hot dogs in the aisles, and every fifteen minutes the cast breaks off from singing to have a fight.

Please note that if you're considering becoming an opera singer you will be required to have a body mass index of less than twenty-five and be under thirty years of age, especially if you are playing a consumptive boho. (Unfortunately, there is still some age discrimination in Heaven, but they're working on that.)

We know that no one with any sense goes to the opera for the realism, the plot, or the believable acting. Opera goers sit through three and a half hours of tedium waiting for the arias. So, in Heaven that's all you get: "O mio babbino caro" from Gianni Schicchi and ""Nessun dorma" from Turandot and then everyone legs it home in time for *Big Brother* (see below).

Ballet

Ballet is like basketball for rich people. Both activities have man-

aged to turn jumping in the air into an art form, and they both require a lot of athletic ability and talent— two things that the majority of humans don't have. In Heaven, in the interests of cultural diversity and broadening both activities' appeal, this synergy is more fully explored, so this season Rudolf Nureyev can be seen playing shooting guard and Wilt Chamberlain's Odette in *Swan Lake* is not to be missed. So far this season Wilt has averaged twenty-nine fouettés and eighteen triple pirouettes per game, and in the locker room after every performance he still finds time to make sweet love to 1.2 women. Imagine that?

Museums

Remember when you were a kid on vacation and your mom dragged you from the beach to take you to a crusty museum for a "wonderful educational experience?" and all you saw was room after room filled with bits of stone and old bones? Well it doesn't have to be that way. In this museum everyone is given a pair of X-ray specs (but not those fake ones you sent off for when you were a kid). These ones allow you to see through clothing and skin, making looking at bones a heck of a lot more entertaining!

Night clubs

If you gave away all your favorite acoustic albums because you thought that your love affair with electronic music was real and would last forever, you'll want to check out the crazy club scene. Well, make that check out the club, but they've managed to pack the authentic club experience into one neat little package. Come down and shake your groove thing! (Shake your groove thing . . .)

Remember, you won't be allowed in with skater shoes, even though the last ten people were just let in barefoot. The inside of this redesigned former church has been fully decked out with a coat check giving away $5 each time you hand over an item, lots of under-lit bars, sticky back-lit walls, and your own velvet-roped VIP area to make you feel super special, where you can sit (imagine that) and nurse your $2 keg of Rochefort Trappistes while you check out the self-conscious posers waving their hands in the air on the dance floor. Add a high-tech lighting rig and a deafening sound system to the mix and in a couple hours you're ready to go home and curl up with a mug of Horlicks.

Television listings

Because Heaven panders to popular taste, TV is even worse here than on earth, with wall to wall reality TV shows. Like the movies, they too are sanitized for your wholesome viewing pleasure. You can even have free spoilers sent directly to your cell phone (which, by the way, get impeccable service even in the clouds!) so that you'll never again be upset by a surprise plot twist. Here's a sample of three of the current most popular reality shows:

Big Brother: Ten monks of above average height spend three months together in an ascetic retreat isolated from the outside world but under the continuous gaze of Jesus Christ. The audience is invited to share in their unbridled conditioning of mind and body in favor of the spirit. Once weekly the public votes to decide which of the nominated housemates has succeeded in cultivating the most balance and depth. At the end of the game, love always wins.

Hell's Got Talent: A devotional talent show that features priests, rabbis, imams, gurus, maharishi, lamas, and other damned spiritual leaders competing for the advertised top prize of a place in Heaven.

Temptation Island: Several religious couples agree to live with a group of really sexy occultists in order to test the strength of their relationship with God and to emphasize the reliability of the Bible and the need for the transformation of an individual's life with faith in Jesus.

SIGHTSEEING

Everything you have heard or read about concerning the beauty of Heaven is only half the story: You could spend an eternity here and still not tire of its delirious assault of sights, sounds, and smells, and its breathtaking, untrammelled vistas (even its trammelled vistas are a sight to behold). It exceeds its reputation as a place where the triple curses of sin, death, and James Blunt have been removed forever.

The urge to travel, to open ourselves up to new experiences, is a basic human desire. As a species, we didn't get where we are today by staying in our huts and watching cable. Humans relish a challenge; it's what makes us better than the animals (that and roll-on deodorant). Whenever an animal has some spare time, it either sleeps or licks itself; it doesn't go exploring for its own sake. But humans are different—they have a wanderlust. They need to experience life beyond their immediate surroundings and to look for greener pastures.

In short, some people are never satisfied. You would think that in Heaven, where every whim is indulged and every desire can be fulfilled, that no one would feel compelled to pack their bags and go sightseeing, or to strap a couple of canoes to the roof of their car and head for the mountains. Oh no! Heaven is littered with restless ingrates who can't sit still for five minutes and have to stamp their authority on their surroundings by tramping around the place taking photos, gathering around maps, and clogging up sidewalks, obstructing all the other angels who are just trying to get on with their afterlives.

If you happen to be one of these stubborn, grass-is-always-greener types, then here are a handful of sights definitely worth checking out. You'll be able to inflict your ignorance on the locals, stop suddenly in the middle of the sidewalk for no reason and point into the air, and complain loudly when you can't find a Starbucks and no one will get upset.

Throne of Glory

Heaven's architecture owes much of its character and appeal to its showcase landmark, the Throne of Glory, which is one of the six things that pre-existed Creation (along with Regis Philbin and the Rolling Stones). It is even more impressive than its description in The Book of Revelation. A masterpiece of anti-Modernism, it is constructed half of fire, half of cornice molding, and hovers in the ether covering an area the size

of Texas. This timeless classic is so large that it even generates its own weather system. The Bible describes how flashes of lightning and peals of divine thunder emanate from it continually, though many religious schisms and wars have arisen over whether or not it has been Scotchgarded.

At the right hand of God sits a TV remote the size of Rhode Island, but the throne itself is mainly reserved for state functions such as the Day of Judgment. For everyday use He prefers a polypropylene egg-cup swivel chair.

The River of Life

Flowing out of the Throne of Glory is the pure River of Life—its holy water is clear as crystal, providing infinite nourishment and refreshment. Just one drop is sufficient to quench the most raging thirst and make you feel instantly revived (unfortunately, not from the dead). If you have a cut or bruise, one drop of this magical elixir heals it upon contact.

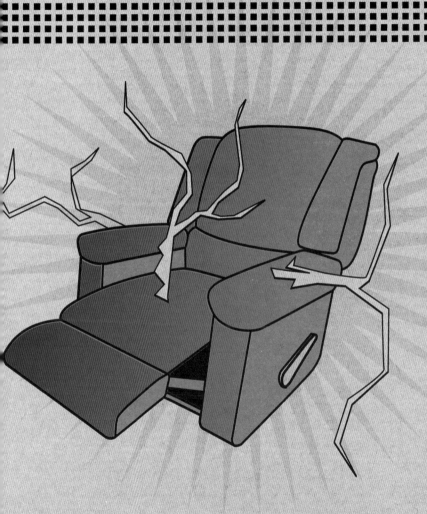

The river continues to be popular for its more traditional uses like baptisms and driving demons out of the possessed. There isn't really much call for exorcisms in Heaven, but mixed with two eggs and tomato juice, it is the best way to get rid of an evil hangover. The water from the River of Life also removes wrinkles, nail varnish, unwanted body hair, stubborn stains, pet odors from curtains and upholstery, and lime scale from toilets and most household appliances.

Graceland

Just because people die and go to Heaven doesn't mean that they stop being wacky worshippers of things that made them happy on earth. Thousands make the pilgrimage each year to visit the heavenly abode of the undisputed King of Rock 'n' Roll. Some hope to catch a unique glimpse into the afterlife of a dead legend, others to renew their wedding vows, while many just gather to eat peanut butter and banana sandwiches and share their hunk-a hunk-a burnin' love with other wig-and-shades-wearing Elvis fanatics. The friendly sales staff at the gift shop next door hope you'll boogie on in after your tour is over. They told me to tell you, "Thank you, thank you very much" in advance.

Garden of Paradise

Many religions depict Heaven as a wonderful garden. Islam describes paradise as a beautiful garden, to which an angel leads you through a gate made of emeralds. Here even the soil smells of expensive perfume, and the rocks and pebbles are made of precious jewels. The birds sing lovely songs and flowers bloom in vibrant colors, and there's even a constant refreshing breeze that is never too hot nor too cold. Hindus believe that the throne of Vishnu (the protector of the Universe and one of their most important gods) is surrounded by white lotus flowers, whose scent can be smelled for miles around. Buddhists imagine the "Pure Land"

91

with sweet-smelling rivers, giant lotus flowers, and gold and jewels literally growing on trees. The ancient Egyptians imagined a heavenly swampland far away to the west called the Field of Reeds. To each his own, right?

However, bear in mind that like any large public amenity, paradise relies on your cooperation to ensure that everyone can enjoy it. So please take a moment to read these terms and conditions carefully:

1. In accordance with the Angels with Disabilities Act, God is working to make paradise accessible to people of all abilities, even rednecks. Call ahead if you are planning to visit for up-to-date information on accessibility, lottery tickets, and styrofoam coolers.

2. Keep off the grass (that goes for harder drugs, too).

3. No dumping (and go to the bathroom before you leave home).

4. Do not take photos in front of the statue of Balto—because there isn't one.

5. No alcoholic beverages allowed on paradise property (unless you are a Methodist, Muslim, or Hindu—these guys sure have some catching up to do).

6. No weapons or firearms allowed. (Feels kind of funny, don't it—enjoying the beauty of nature without trying to kill it?)

7. No swimming or radio controlled boats allowed on the River of Life. "Fishing of men" is acceptable, except where prohibited.

8. Skate at your own risk only in areas where the ice is thick enough and completely free from Canadians.

9. All children eight years of age or younger must be accompanied by a cacophony of repetitive blathering and unnecessary energy expenditure.

10. Bikers, Rollerbladers, roller skaters, and skateboarders are prohibited at all times, with or without their equipment.

"SOMETIMES I LIE AWAKE AT NIGHT, AND I ASK, 'WHERE HAVE I GONE WRONG?' THEN A VOICE SAYS TO ME, 'THIS IS GOING TO TAKE MORE THAN ONE NIGHT.'"

—Charlie Brown

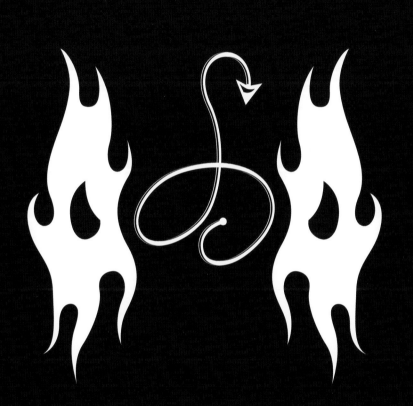

DESTINATION: HELL

Shame on you! Your ugliness wasn't just skin deep then. Bet you didn't imagine in a million years that you'd end up here.

Welcome to Hell, the place of eternal damnation, and of incessant wailing and gnashing of teeth; where five minutes can feel like at least ten or fifteen minutes and the hours really drag. More often than not, time literally stands still.

That's the first thing that you will notice about Hell. Well actually, the first thing will probably be all the cuckoo clocks (It has always been an open secret that Satan and the Swiss have a long standing arrangement). They are here as a constant and unwelcome reminder of the sluggish passage of time.

We expect you're keen to find out what's in store for you here. All in good time, my friend, all in good time. But before you bemoan the loss of paradise, here's some stale food for thought:

There was once a Rabbi who wanted to see Heaven and Hell, so God issued him a one-day visitor pass, and he found himself standing in front of a door with no name. He knocked on the door, and when it opened he peered inside. He saw a great banquet hall with tables laden with all kinds of food. People sat at the tables holding chopsticks that were eight feet long; all of them were hungry and miserable, and cursed God, while their stomachs rumbled in a cacophony of blasphemous despair.

They desperately wanted to eat but the chopsticks were too long. Each time someone tried to get something into their mouths, the food fell onto the floor where it was devoured by ravenous dogs. Not a single morsel passed anyone's lips. Immediately, the Rabbi realized that he was in Hell, and quickly closed the door in horror.

Soon, he found himself standing in front of another closed door. Once again he knocked, and once again it opened to reveal an identical banquet hall full of people, with tables covered with the most incredible fare. Everyone had the same eight-foot chopsticks, but they were all smiling. This was Heaven, but the Rabbi couldn't understand why everyone was so happy, since their circumstances were identical to that suffered by the miserable wretches he had just seen in Hell. Then all of a sudden it became clear.

At the far end of the room Jesus rose to his feet. He was wearing dark sunglasses and a bed sheet knotted to form a makeshift toga. Suddenly he punched the air and shouted "food fight!" and everyone started hurling food at each other. What a bunch of losers, *thought the Rabbi and slammed the door. If he had delayed a second longer he would have been hit in the face by an egg.*

The moral of the story is that sometimes it's better to starve than to live with morons.

WHAT THE FAQ?

Lucifer, Beelzebub, Iblis; no matter what you call him, Satan generally gets a bad rap. Some folks blame him for all that's wrong with the world. Others blame either the Dixie Chicks or Dubya. Either way, the Devil regularly scores highly in surveys where people are asked to name a scapegoat or something evil. But is he all bad or merely misunderstood? Is his endless quest to harvest human souls really evil, or just something he does because there wasn't a youth center in his neighborhood when he was growing up? And is Hell really as bad as all that? In this chapter, we attempt to answer some of your burning questions (no pun intended). However, since this is Hell, we can't vouch for the reliability of any of the information.

Is Hell really as bad as all that?

When it comes to evil there are no easy answers. If you learned anything on earth it should be that there are shades of gray, and good and evil isn't black and white. To decide how bad Hell is it really depends on what you compare it to. For instance, it is still way better than living in Canada or Mexico (but don't forget that the winner of the rat race is still a rat).

Ten reasons why Hell is better than Canada

1. There are no Canadians.

2. There's no ice and, thus, no hockey.

3. You won't get arrested for burning effigies of Celine Dion, Martin Short, or Jim Carrey in public.

4. You won't get deported or eaten by a bear.

5. Nobody cares about clean air, education, or affordable healthcare.

6. The taxes are lower and the gas and beer are cheaper.

7. Wearing lumber jackets, funny hats, and mukluk-style boots is a punishment rather than a fashion statement.

8. Only 95 percent of its inhabitants are alcoholics.

9. Nobody owns a snow blower or lives in an igloo (see 1 and 2).

10. A smaller proportion of Hell is uninhabitable.

Ten reasons why Hell is better than Mexico

1. It's cooler.

2. There's no cacti, Telmex, or Nike sweatshops.

3. The mail service is more reliable.

4. You're less likely to get mugged.

5. You can drink the water . . . kind of (see below).

6. There are no tourists.

7. There is no social inequality: In Hell everyone lives in a dusty hut with a tin roof and no windows.

8. More people try to escape from Mexico each year.

9. It is easier to survive in Hell.

10. Mexico is a corrupt oligarchy controlled by a bunch of drug dealers; Hell is merely a secular dictatorship.

Can Satan read our minds?

Don't believe everything you think. There is no biblical evidence that the Devil can read our minds, although there are plenty of examples of God reading our thoughts, for example: "The Lord searches all hearts, and understands every intent of our thoughts" (1 Chronicles 21:8) and "The Lord knows the thoughts of man, that they are a mere breath" (Psalms 94:11). Bearing this in mind, who would you prefer to spend eternity with? That said, if Satan wants to know your thoughts, he can always beat them out of you.

What's the weather like?

The heat is deceptively strong—one hour of sunbathing will give you a bone-deep tan. A light sweater is unnecessary, even in the evening, when the temperature falls to just below one million degrees Fahrenheit. Avoid man-made fibers, which will melt and stick to your body, sometimes creating a very uncomfortable skin rash. Always travel with an umbrella or a large trash bag. It won't protect you from the heat or the rain (huge globules of boiling sulfur that fall from above, leap out of the ground, and are driven at you sideways by unremitting winds), but it is a useful container with which to collect your peeling skin.

Can I drink the water?

The water here is remarkably free from microbes, but there's a very good reason for that: It's boiling. You face a difficult choice between a permanent feeling of thirst and severe dehydration—and cooking your internal organs.

If two heads are better than one, why do they try to separate conjoined twins?

So that when they grow up they can pay the IRS twice.

Just how many ways are there to skin a cat?

Thirty-eight.

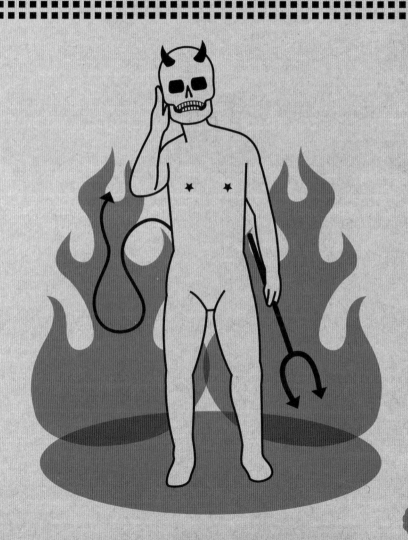

If God helps those who help themselves, what's the point of helping others?
Exactly.

Can I smoke in Hell?
Residents are not allowed to smoke while being tortured, and they may smoke only in a designated room or outside (unless it is the direct result of being burned alive). You are entitled to take a fifteen-minute break in mid-June and another in December, during which you may choose to smoke. You have no statutory entitlement to other breaks, even to visit the bathroom, however, since most of the punishments involve repeated evisceration, you are unlikely to require a toilet break.

The health and safety rationale behind the annual two-breaks policy is flawless in its logic: Research has shown that tired people have accidents, so by decreasing breaks the risk of accidents increases. Your statement of terms and conditions does allow a short daily lunch break, but you will probably feel pressured not to take it, since there is a culture here of not taking lunch breaks, and if you do, sarcastic comments get made. In any case, the food is so vile that you will spend most of your time in the bathroom throwing up. However, you are allowed unlimited herbal tea.

Why can't I get a good cup of coffee in Hell?
Economies of scale: just as Starbucks stopped using good coffee beans when they moved out of Seattle, Satan hasn't experimented with a new blend since he invented the Internet. Though things aren't much better upstairs—Never order the drip coffee in Heaven. God may have a reputation for being eternally self-giving, but He is usually so busy talking to Pat Robertson and Jerry Falwell that He hardly ever has time to change the pot.

What will I look like?

Your skin will be saggy and wrinkled beyond belief as you're constantly dealing with flesh burns down under. Other than that, for the most part you'll look like everyone else—clinically depressed and careworn by excruciating pain. It is vital that tortures excoriate the body, so everyone keeps the one they had on earth, but it resembles a more degraded version of their earthly selves. Bald people have shinier heads, short people have their legs amputated below the knees, and glamor models are given access to unlimited plastic surgery.

Will we have sex?

You will have lots and lots of sex, and all of it against your will. Did you know that rape and pillage are condoned in the Bible?

In Numbers 31:7-18 after the Israelites had defeated the Midianites in battle, Moses was furious because they had let all the women live. He commanded them: "Now kill all the boys and all the women who have slept with a man. Only the young girls who are virgins may live; you may keep them for yourselves."

And what about Zechariah 14:1-2: "Behold, the day of the Lord cometh, and thy spoil shall be divided in the midst of thee. For I will gather all nations against Jerusalem to battle; and the city shall be taken, and the houses rifled, and the women ravished; and half of the city shall go forth into captivity, and the residue of the people shall not be cut off from the city."

Nice.

If every dog has his day, which ones have already had theirs? And do they know it? And if they do, what have they got left to live for?
God only knows.

If beggars can't be choosers, what happens if you choose to become a beggar and then immediately change your mind?

You're screwed.

Why did God create humans if he knew some of them would go to Hell?

According to Matthew 25:41, Hell was "prepared for the Devil and his angels." It was not created for man. God didn't want anybody to go to Hell, but once he had created it, it was inevitable that some humans would end up living there. The same thing happened after He created Atlanta, Detroit, and Arkansas.

Why did Satan fall from Heaven?

At one time not only was Satan in God's favor, he was his roomie, but it seems that stable relationships are only meant for horses. Satan covered the walls with pentagrams and Marilyn Manson posters, never cleaned the toilet, and always "borrowed" money to pay the rent. At first God wanted to avoid a confrontation and He decided that they just needed an adjustment period. However, a few thousand years later Satan was still stealing God's shampoo, bringing chicks back at all hours of the night, and occasionally drawing Hitler-esque moustaches on His face while He was asleep. Finally God said enough is enough.

It came to a head after Satan borrowed the Ethernet cable from God's computer without asking and ate an entire batch of gingerbread cookies that He spent the whole afternoon baking. Since God is omniscient he knew that Satan was lying through his sociopathic teeth. Mind you, he clearly didn't foresee that Satan was going to eat all the cookies, unless he deliberately engineered the whole thing ex nihilo so that he could have an excuse for losing his cool. Either way, he was

annoyed at himself more than anything, so he did what all right-minded deities would have done in the circumstances: He threw a Biblical fit and shouted "How art thou fallen from heaven, O Lucifer, son of the morning! How art thou cut down to the ground, which didst weaken the nations! For thou hast messed up my stuff for the last time. I am sick and tired of cleaning up after you, you slob; you don't appreciate me and, for Christ's sake, you can't even pee without hitting the bathroom walls!"

And so it came to pass that Satan was booted out of Heaven and was cast down into the Abyss, and they never spoke to each other again. God was so angry he didn't even forward Satan's mail.

THE SEVEN DEADLY SINS

The Roman Catholic Church divided sin into two principal categories: "venial," which are relatively minor and could be forgiven through any sacrament of the Church; and the more severe mortal sin (or Deadly Sin), which, when committed, really messed with your head and created the threat of eternal damnation unless either absolved through the sacrament of confession, or otherwise forgiven through paying wheelbarrow loads of money to the church (called "selling indulgences"—a process very similar to selling carbon "offsets" today).

The punishment you receive in Hell depends on which of the Seven Deadly Sins are your all-time favorites. These are a classification of vices that were originally used in early Christian teachings to scare the crap out of everyone with the constant reminder of their tendency to sin. They were originally cooked up in the sixth century A.D. by Pope Gregory the Great, and he believed that pride was the worst of all since he said it bred all the others.

The Ten Commandments had been written on two unwieldy tablets: Greg wanted a more portable format for his venial vision. Hence, the Seven Deadly Sins were born, a user friendly guide to the avoidance of sin. The holy men whittled down their many discoveries to: Pride, Envy, Avarice, Wrath, Lust, Gluttony, and Sloth. This was reiterated in the thirteenth century by St. Thomas Aquinas in his *Summa Theologica* and the Seven Deadly Sins have formed a moral compass for earthly sinners ever since.

They're all explained here, along with their respective punishments:

Pride

Pride is the cultivation, preservation, or exaltation of self. It is expressed in vanity, self-advancement, all forms of religious fundamentalism, or feeling superior to others. So whether you've strapped five pounds of plastic explosives to your chest and run into a market in Basra, or you look down on those whose lifetime goal is to own a fireworks stand, your punishment in Hell will be the same: being broken on the wheel.

This gruesome torture was very popular in Europe during the Middle Ages. First you are stretched out with your limbs tied to the spokes of a large wagon wheel. The wheel is then turned by one of the Devil's advocates and a large hammer or iron bar is used to break your bones, several times for each limb. Afterward, your shattered limbs are braided through the spokes of the wheel which is hoisted onto a tall pole, so that birds can eat you alive.

Envy

Envy is wanting other people's stuff and that can include anything from one man's goat to another woman's boob job. So if you regularly drool over the pages of *OK!* magazine you can expect to freeze your desires away by being encased in sub-zero glacial water for all eternity. As you look around at all the other envious souls trapped with you, no doubt you'll have a gripe about the temperature of your bit of water. (Seriously, you need to chill out.)

Avarice

Avarice is the miserly desire to gain and hoard wealth. Whether you're in the Forbes 400 or you shop in thrift stores and craft your own Christmas gifts, you're still a greedy tightwad who deserves to be boiled in oil.

Wrath

Wrath is another favorite of religious fundamentalists. If you suffer from frequent temper tantrums then you've probably just arrived here after suffering from a big, fat heart attack. Your punishment is to be torn apart, limb by limb. That'll serve you right for thinking your bad attitude is everyone else's problem.

Lust

Lust is an excessive craving for the pleasures of the body, for which you can look forward to being roasted by fire and brimstone. The scriptures aren't clear about how much excessive craving is permissible before it tips over into unwanted lust. As a general rule: Voyeuring your neighbor's wife taking a shower is okay; whipping out your camcorder is not.

Gluttony

Gluttony is an inordinate desire to consume more than that which one requires, or in layman's terms: being a selfish little bastard. You'll be forced to eat rats, toads, snakes, and spiders (which, technically, isn't much of a punishment if you're French or Chinese).

Sloth

Sloth is the avoidance of physical or spiritual work. Whether your necrophiliac lover dumps you for being too passive or you can't get off the sofa to fetch another beer, your punishment is being thrown into a snake pit. That should get you moving, you big slob.

MEET THE PEOPLE

When you first arrive in Hell there are a few formalities to get out of the way. They can be quite inconvenient, but remember that they are nothing compared to the torture that awaits you. [Insert Dr. Evil laughter again.] These few preliminary procedures insure you have everything you need for a totally miserable stay, and highlight any fears or problems you may have such as a phobia about spiders or an embarrassing or debilitating medical complaint. This is so that a personalized program of torture can be implemented to exploit your weaknesses.

First you will be asked to empty your pockets. Your personal effects will be carefully listed before being incinerated. Next you will be given a full body cavity examination lasting for two hours, after which you will have a shower followed by a more thorough cavity exam. Then you will be allocated a number or "mark of the beast." You can choose from any one of the eleven designs that, at the time of writing, currently adorn the body of Angelina Jolie, ranging from a large tribal dragon to the geographical map coordinates accurately detailing the four hidden levels in Tomb Raider Anniversary Edition. Or you may opt for the more traditional 666 branded with a red hot iron on the most sensitive part of your body. This is the Carina, the point of bifurcation of the trachea which is supplied by the tenth cranial nerve and thoracic nerves. However, for convenience most likely you'll be burned on the second most sensitive part of the body: ball sack (for men) or earlobe (for women).

Satan recognizes that being sent to Hell can be a traumatic and often distressing experience for many people. For this reason there are a number of peer support programs run specifically by the damned for the damned. The most popular of these is the guardian angel listener program. A guardian angel is an inhabitant of Hell who has been allocated to individual souls. At any time during your stay you can discuss your problems with them. The guardian angels are specially trained to ignore your concerns and to make fun of you if there is anything you don't understand. You can tell them anything in total confidence, but they'll broadcast your secrets to everyone else anyway.

Meet your maker's enemy

In order to establish your place in the pecking order, walk up to the biggest and meanest looking person you can find and kick him in the nuts. He will then hit you so hard that all your teeth will fall out, which is still preferable to the pain and hassle of slow decay through stress and an inadequate diet. Congratulations: you've just met Satan. Don't be scared though. He likes being kicked in the nuts, but what he loves more is getting even. When you regain consciousness, the customary response is "Thank you, Sir. Please may I have another?" and Satan is always happy to oblige. Expect these initial formalities to last for a few months.

After he has broken you in, Satan won't seem like such a bad old stick after all. That probably has more to do with Stockholm syndrome than anything, because he is a firm believer in tough hate (as opposed to tough love). When he finally relaxes his guard, he will reveal some of his charm that you found so irresistible on earth.

Do agnostics get into Hell?

Atheism takes a position that either affirms the nonexistence of gods or rejects theism, whereas agnosticism posits that gods, along with the rest of reality, are inherently unknowable. For this reason, you are more likely to go to Hell for being an agnostic than an atheist because God tries to avoid smart people who question the nature of subjective experience. This makes Him so paranoid that He starts to doubt His own existence. And since God is probably the leading proponent of proof by design (the belief that the magnificent order of things is proof enough that He created it), He is understandably reluctant to face the possibility that He might be the only thing in the Universe that isn't invited to the cosmic party, that He is a mere meme in the collective minds of true believers, and that the Universe came into existence and continues to thrive independently of Him. You can see His point: If you were God, wouldn't that thought keep you awake at night?

Celebrity hellions

You will see lots of famous faces here, from Moses, Abraham, and Lot's daughters to Southern Baptists. In fact, nearly everyone in Hell is famous or infamous, because you can't lead a really despicable life without achieving a degree of notoriety, nor become really famous during your lifetime without it turning you into a bit of a jerk.

You'll see the inevitable rash of cruel dictators, from Torquemada to Stalin, and scores of deceased executives from Enron, Halliburton, Andersen, KMPG, and Merrill Lynch. Sigmund Freud is here (at the request of his mother), Lizzie Borden (at the request of her

father), and the Marquis de Sade (at the request of his hamster).

All in all, the roster of lost souls is disappointingly predictable, although there are a few welcome surprises, including Lenny Bruce, John Belushi, and Bill Hicks.

The twenty-five people you meet in Hell

Hell is the perfect place to settle old scores. As you would expect, there is an ongoing East Coast-West Coast feud, which escalated from a battle of words to a bloody war, fronted by Tupac and Biggie Smalls. It seems they just can't let old wounds heal.

Hell is the place to get even, and where others will want to get even with you, from people you cut in line at Subway to the innocents you bludgeoned and strangled to death (if you're Ted Bundy). Most of them are ready to take part in some five-knuckle philosophy, but you may run into some old friends:

1. Your fourth-grade geography teacher who used to throw white-board markers at his students to stop them from falling asleep. Now that you've both got plenty of time on your hands, he's itching to explain to you about the subtleties of glacial erosion and ox-bow lakes.

2. The cute woman you chatted with on a bus in 2001 who told you that *Pearl Harbor* was the best movie she had ever seen, and made you promise her that you would see it that very evening. Suffice it to say that you have some unfinished business with that delusional lady.

3. Dr. Clement Okon, the Nigerian civil servant who persuaded you to e-mail him your bank account details so that he could transfer you $21,320,000,000.

4. The surgeon who agreed to operate on Zac Efron when he was admitted to Cedars-Sinai Medical Center in Los Angeles for

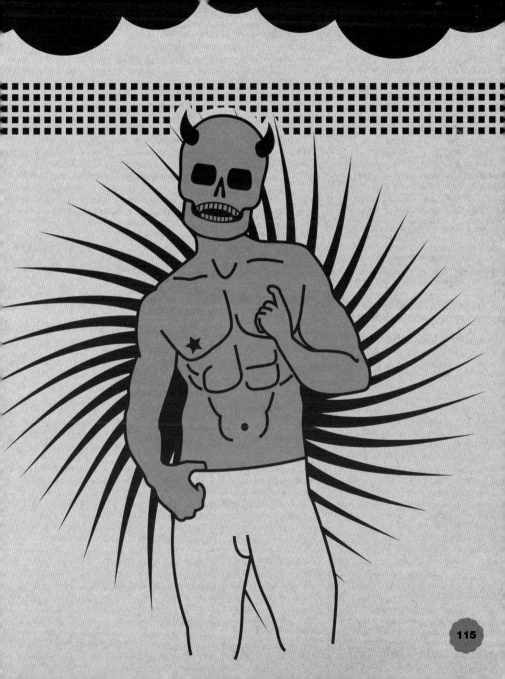

an emergency life-saving appendectomy.

5. That image consultant trainee who plucked your eyebrows so badly that you spent three months looking totally demonic, and everyone thought you were the bastard lovechild of Vince Vaughn and Marcia Cross.

6. Smokers who left their ashtrays in the middle of the floor, or balanced on the arm of the couch.

7. Grown women with hair so long they could sit on it.

8. Everyone who said "aks" instead of "ask." Like "Can I aks you a question?" Gaaaaaah! Seriously? The word has three letters and you still get it wrong!

9. Everyone who ever muttered "sarcasm is the lowest form of wit." They're annoying and wrong: Spewing out trite moralistic aphorisms like "sarcasm is the lowest form of wit" is the lowest form of wit.

10. Guys who kept pressing their pectoral muscles to feel how big and hard they were, especially the ones who didn't even realize they were doing it because they were so vain that it had become an ingrained subconscious tick.

11. People who had an online domain name you needed and then did nothing with it.

12. People who couldn't stop talking about their personal relationships with God and how much they love Him.

13. Morons who would pull out their iPhones and pretend to check the time, when all they were doing was showing them off.

14. People who were excessively happy all the time on earth.

15. Posers who claimed that Macs "are just better" than PCs but, when pressed, they couldn't think of a single reason why.

16. Female gym rats who wore a full face of make up to work out.

17. Anyone who said their favorite band was some new group that had just released its first single.

18. People who trusted their antivirus computer software unthinkingly.

19. Cry babies who got all passive-aggressive and wouldn't talk to you for weeks because you forgot to send them a birthday card.

20. Rich SOBs who took items of clothing to the dry cleaners when the care labels clearly stated that they were machine washable.

21. People who posted lame footage of themselves doing dumb things on YouTube, and then protested when they became Internet phenomenons.

22. Rich celebrities who reinvented themselves every five years and everyone sucked it up and praised them for being so ahead of the curve.

23. People who used any of the following phrases: "At the end of the day," "So I turned round and said . . ." or "yourself and myself" (instead of "you" and "me") and politicians who say "make no mistake . . ." or "let's be absolutely clear" just before they tell a big fat lie.

24. People who got mad when you borrowed their stuff without asking permission.

25. Anyone who owned a Fabergé egg.

ETIQUETTE

Adapting to the regime here can be unsettling; it's a culture unto itself, with many new rules and regulations, routines, and social hierarchies. In Hell common courtesy is in short supply, since it didn't come easily to its wretched inhabitants when they were alive, let alone while they face an eternity of barbaric torture inflicted by fantastical creatures beyond their worst nightmares. Imagine for a moment having your inner ear eaten away by a malign entity with the body of a slug, anal cysts the size of melons, and the head of Rush Limbaugh. Well, earthly horrors like these are nothing compared to what awaits us in Hell.

Since most rules governing socially acceptable conduct are followed either for self-advancement or from the fear of punishment, in Hell, the former is impossible and the latter is arbitrary and never-ending. There are few incentives here to show kindness and respect toward your fellow companions. Tempers run high and at times common decency can be hard to find, but do not despair. The human spirit can flourish and triumph in the face of the darkest adversity. Follow the social rules outlined below to keep safe and stay on the scene.

Meeting and greeting
In this culture it isn't essential to maintain good eye contact, but you should still watch out for any sudden body movements, and use your peripheral vision to make sure no one jumps you from behind.

The ancient origin behind the common handshake is to demonstrate the absence of a weapon. In Hell this imperative is more literal than symbolic; the customary greeting is to give the other person a quick frisk. When you are satisfied that they won't cut your lips and tongue from your head with a concealed linoleum knife, you can take a few steps back and engage them in small talk.

Body language
The most important rule of social interaction is to get noticed. Hell is a full-time red carpet event (minus the cameras, the carpet, and Cameron Diaz), and it's in your best interests to let everyone else know that when you make an entrance, business is about to pick up big time.

Socially, Hell is like a super-maximum security prison in Bel Air.

Being famous is the only social currency so it pays to draw attention to yourself as much as you can. The more you can wash your dirty laundry in public and give the impression of being a shallow, superficial, and image-obsessed meltdown media maven, the more respect you will gain.

Dress
Everyone in Hell wears regulation Guantánamo-style orange jumpsuits, red Halloween devil horns, a clip-on pointy tail, and a T-shirt with the slogan, YOU DON'T HAVE TO BE IRREDEEMABLY EVIL TO WORK HERE, BUT IT HELPS. These clothes are issued immediately after the third and final strip search.

Conversation
Always begin a conversation by checking your watch and saying something like "I have something really important I need to take

care of in two minutes," to show that the person you're talking to is basically a waste of your time. It will make that person feel rushed and self-conscious and you'll look and feel very powerful in the process.

People here love talking about themselves, so try to begin every sentence with "I" and whenever the topic of conversation drifts away from you, bring it lumbering back by telling an inappropriate personal anecdote of tenuous relevance. Only give opinions on subjects about which you are completely unknowledgeable to ensure that your sweeping generalizations cause maximum offense. One-upping others in conversations is allowed and encouraged.

When making small talk, always remember that your opinions override those of others. Be inflexible and subordinate their feelings, try to put them ill at ease, and make them feel self-conscious in gen-eral. You can use anything from personal observations such as "I see you've put on a few pounds" or "Gross! You have something in your teeth" and then keep telling them they didn't get it as they pick and scratch away, to full-blown trash-talk like "Talk to the left 'cause you sure ain't right!" while shoving your left hand in front of the other person's face, invading their personal space and then some.

Name dropping is always good, and, when used skilfully, can elevate your social standing in even the most banal circumstances. For example, saying "Hermann Göring helped me pick out this couch" works a hell of a lot better than "I got this half-price in the IKEA sale."

Table manners
Parties and other social functions are a great way to let your hair down, but in Hell they are a non-starter because everyone tries to be the last to arrive and the first

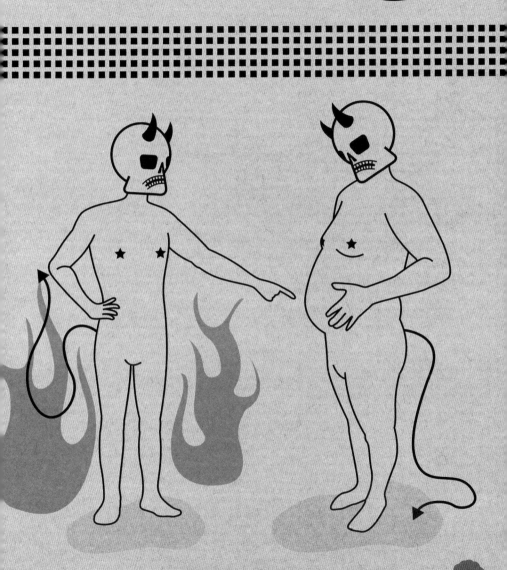

to leave. This means that no one turns up and every event usually has to be cancelled.

Restaurant service is worse than that at a Shanghai city diner. Attract a waiter's attention by making eye contact and raising your eyebrows. You can also raise your index finger after you catch your waiter's eye, or cover your arms with a criss-cross of track-lines and scratches.

Before your meal arrives, it is customary to go the bathroom and throw up. If anyone asks why your teeth are falling out and your breath stinks worse than a bum's,

glare and tell them to mind their own business.

During a meal, blowing and/or picking your nose, vomiting, and sneezing without covering your mouth is acceptable as long as it is done discreetly.

Eat and pass plates of food with your right hand, and stick your fingers down your throat with the other.

When the bill arrives, it is customary for everyone to fight to avoid paying by claiming that they only ordered mineral water and a salad.

ACCOMMODATIONS

Travellers here have plenty to agonize over in this undiscovered country where health standards are the lowest of anywhere in the uncivilized underworld. If you want definitive proof that Satan is more than a cosmic metaphor, that Hell isn't a mere state of mind, and that sin and human moral failings do not go unnoticed, take a gander at the deplorable accommodations that are offered here.

The establishments you choose to go to during your time in Hell can make or break your entire experience. It's good to do your research and find the option that best suits your own needs. You may choose to pay for your earthly crimes by being buried upside-down in a hole, with your feet on fire; or perhaps you require a resort that offers relentless interruptions such as rowdy morons vomiting outside your door in the wee hours. But like many sinners, you want an extended stay at the lowest brochure rate while enjoying a basic level of discomfort. Here is a selection of some of the best that Hell has to offer while you settle down to an unvaried program of relentless punishment and torture.

Hotel Paramount

Hotel Paramount is an expensive two-star hotel in the central area of Hell. Its twelve rooms offer clean and basic accommodations at very inflated prices, as well as a skeleton staff. But what, realistically, can you expect for so much money? Breakfast is not particularly good, though if you're Italian you'll be in your element: orange juice, tea/coffee, a tough fresh roll, and a selection of plastic-wrapped snacks. There is black mold growing in the shower and the TV is broken. However, this is the most luxurious hotel in Hell, and if you think this is bad, keep reading. From here on in, things can only get much, much worse.

Tortura Grande

If you're looking for somewhere to totally relax, unwind, and listen to your thoughts, you've come to the wrong place. When you're not being disturbed by the shrill arguments, raucous parties, and toilet-flushing antics of the other guests, the total lack of silence is punctuated by a symphony of chattering pipework and the intermittent whirring of power tools, although it never becomes apparent what they are being used for.

Just when you think the aural medley is dying down, cringe afresh at the sound of passionate lovemaking drifting through the flimsy, paper-thin partitioned walls as a faceless couple in the suite across the corridor attempt to document

an unwritten chapter in the McKinsey report. When you call the front desk to complain, you will be put on hold and then the receptionist will forget to pick up the phone again. On the positive side: You won't be bothered by traffic noise, which is usually drowned out by the sound of kittens being flayed alive in the lobby.

Circle Five

This intimidating retreat is set among seventeen acres of dirty marshland where the souls of the wrathful lie trapped for eternity. Sample the bank-side restaurant where you can dine with your toes in the sand, your feet on the veranda, and your liver hanging from a nearby palm tree. This place achieves a masterful combination of both minor and major irritations. For example, after discovering that the iron in your room is broken, head to the lounge area where a succubus will rip your head off (free of charge).

L'Inferno

On earth the temperature of a hotel room is only designed to kill; here this principle is taken one step further. Built into the mountains overlooking the lake of fire, the setting is spectacular. Relax in the shady grounds, while the scent of brimstone drifts by on the breeze. Enjoy pre-dinner drinks in the fireplace, or feel the skin peeling off your face as coffee is poured on you in the garden. Take pleasure in a post-prandial volcanic lava treatment and then cool off in a boiling spring. The smell of freshly baked human flesh will wake you up each morning—in the kitchen, talented chef Idi Amin creates culinary interest from the local people, and in the evening offers up an unforgettable family carvery.

Sartre's

Sartre's offers all the excitement of watching a pensioner doing the shopping at Wal*Mart. If you were ever in doubt that existence precedes essence, put your feet up and allow the negation of being to wash over you. Overlooking the endless abyss, this one-of-a-kind resort offers an ideal setting for total existential crisis, with none of the earthly displacement activities to distract you from the chock-full meaningless of human existence. Not for you the ugly frenzy of complimentary fruit bowls, power showers, cable TV, and toilet paper folded into an arrow, to protect you from the all-consuming horror of cognitive dissonance.

Old Barn

Your stay in eternal sorrow is perfectly complemented by this venue. This hotel underwent an extensive renovation to preserve the historical characteristics and to retrofit its facilities so that they are now woefully out-of-date to ensure that your comfort and enjoyment are very low down on the list of priorities. The establishment oozes Old World charm, which is apparent the moment you are greeted by the mahogany-panelled receptionist. Each room overlooks and is overlooked by everyone else's room, and every other room except yours is occupied by delegates from a telemarketing conference. Visitors are expected to complain at the office between the hours of 7 a.m. and 11 p.m. daily.

Brown's

This elegant colonic-style mansion has all the sophistication of a frat party and is the architectural epitome of rectal waste. Set within its own working Victorian sewer, overlooking the river of excrement from Dante's eighth circle, the atmosphere is discreetly rank. The color scheme throughout is pale cappuccino. The rooms are tastelessly decorated in period style using soiled toilet paper. When you check in you are proudly presented with a complimentary can of economy-sized Lysol. Each room has stunning uninterrupted views of the air-conditioning fans of neighboring hotels. While you are out and about, the attentive cleaning staff will break in and ransack your apartment.

One Season Hotel
Abandon hope, all who enter here. You couldn't ask for less invigorating surroundings since every room exceeds expectations of discomfort, and is dominated by a floor-to-ceiling chandelier. The walls are so thin the guest next door will ask you to lower the brightness on your TV. There is a copy of the Gideon's Bible in every drawer and a Starbucks at the end of every corridor. Everywhere you turn you will see spoiled natural beauty; even breakfast consists of exposed beams and brickwork. As you eat your dinner, atmospheric music is supplied by Hate Forest, a Ukrainian Black Metal band, whose lyrics are heavily influenced by Slavic mythology and Conservative Revolutionary ideology.

Mulligan's
Mulligan's is a vast ugly pile of brown brick that has definitely seen better days. It is also a bottom-of-the-line, all-inclusive golf condo with three courses. The only things that aren't included are the holes, so there's no chance to improve your handicap, apart from having parts of your body hacked off by rebellious angels.

Palais Thermidor
In the heart of the City of Woe, the Palais Thermidor is a fascinating thermal resort where you can enjoy the feeling of turning back the clock to a time before clocks were invented. Nowhere is the meticulous attention to detail evident, and every modern convenience imaginable has been overlooked. It's difficult to find green spaces in Hell, so Thermidor's parched garden is a delightfully predictable disappointment, formed as it is with yellowish-brown yew hedging and surrounded by phallic topiary.

RESTAURANTS AND EATERIES

When Leonidas, king of the Spartans, shouted, "Tonight we dine in Hell!" he wouldn't have been so upbeat if he had known what was in store. The food in Hell is unappetizing at best, and at worst, bilious and totally inedible. It doesn't matter which of the eateries you choose, you can guarantee you'll end the evening blowing chunks, regretting all of the sins you ever committed and wishing you were alive.

There is a pitiable choice of dining to repel every gourmand and to encourage the frequent ejection of the contents of the stomach through the mouth and nose. We've compiled this shortlist of some of the most spectacularly inadequate venues to encourage you to eat somewhere else. Most of them are situated within easy walking distance of nowhere in particular, since Hell is a bleak and featureless landscape with nothing of interest.

Le Blearghh

Le Blearghh is a place where the worlds of food, culture, and campylobacter converge. The service is negligent yet obtrusive, and the surroundings manage to be effortlessly uninspiring; the atmosphere is always buzzing (mainly with flies).

Throughout his short career, untalented head chef Yves Erpe has consistently ignored the most basic of food hygiene standards and boasts to have trained in some of the most unsanitary kitchens on earth, many of which were recommended for closure under his stewardship.

Yves has the highest standards which he consistently fails to meet. The lack of integrity of his ingredients and the blithe arrogance with which he operates has placed him head and shoulders below his contemporaries. He maintains this utter lack of pedigree with a series of dishes that will send you home with intestinal cramps: pubic lice bisque; fillets of red mullet left out of the fridge overnight; and baby veal stuffed with *Clostridium botulinum*. Says Yves of his unique cooking style, "I haven't killed anyone yet; but hey, I'm only twenty-three."

Rude

This delightfully charmless little bistro offers a dining experience that contrives to be both cheerless and alienating. An evening here simply isn't complete.

On arrival you are immediately made to feel unwelcome in a cramped and woefully under-staffed bar area, and every effort has been spared to ensure that your discomfort grows steadily throughout the evening. This is due in no small part to the indifferent staff, the clinical brightness of the undiffused overhead lighting, and the image-conscious clientele who are too busy looking around to pay any attention to the food.

As soon as your appetizers arrive you will be informed that your table has been double-booked, and you will spend the rest of your meal playing beat the clock. The bland food is complemented perfectly by the lackluster wine list with perfunctory assistance from a witless sommelier.

Rude is particularly popular with celebrities from film, television, fashion, publishing, and advertising. In a recent interview the proprietor said, "There is a real gap in the market for simple unappetizing food served in a competitive and self-conscious environment."

Apollo's

This watering hole has long been associated with two of the biggest names in the restaurant business: rectal prolapse and ulcerative colitis. It has established a reputation for contemporary Greek fast food using ingredients of the highest quality. Ambrosia, the magical substance that conferred immortality on the gods of Greek mythology, features prominently on the menu; it's also on the walls, floor, and tablecloths.

Apollo's ethos has always been to take the finest ingredients and ruin them with improper storage and inept cooking. It recently won the prestigious "Irritable Bowel Award" due to its consistently low expectations and beatable service—definitely a destination to be missed if you value your gastrointestinal tract.

The signature dish is the Apollo donner: finely minced ambrosia, nectar, and spices are pressed together into a cylindrical shape with unidentified meat objects, sawdust, bone chippings, dirt-filled fingernails, dripping sweat, and lots of hair. It is then spit-roasted vertically until the center is a festering mass of bacterial contagion and then served with shredded lettuce in lukewarm pita bread.

Diabolo's

When you're running a successful business the Devil is always in the detail, but here this is literally true: Satan personally picked out the curtains and hand-stitched the scalloped lace fringing onto all the tablecloths. This quaint English restaurant is a beautiful stone building erected during the Middle Ages, remodeled during The Reformation, before being completetly demolished in the 1950s and rebuilt with steel and concrete. There is a friendly informal atmosphere, as evidenced by the cheery wait staff, who chain

smoke and fart loudly while they work. All the food is prepared daily, and served up the following week; however, according to many frequent diners, it offers the best Dover sole in Hell. In fact the proprietor is so confident of this accolade that he proudly boasts if you can find Dover sole anywhere else, he'd like to know about it.

The Bloody Stool

A headline in a prominent magazine recently reported, "The Bloody Stool has got it all." The magazine was the *Health Inspector's Gazette*, and it was referring to food-borne microorganisms, toxins, and parasites. Food poisoning typically strikes within hours or days of eating contaminated food; in this establishment it hits you while you're reading the menu. Even the rats in the kitchen suffer frequent bouts of diarrhea, and the cockroaches are in renal failure. On the positive side, wherever you are sitting in the restaurant you will be afforded a spectacular view of the restrooms,

so when you need to toss your cookies you'll know where to run.

The Big Yack Shack

The Big Yack Shack is an ideal place to meet friends but a terrible place to eat. The head chef likes experimenting with new flavors and exotic spices, but none of them reach the food. Consequently, the Shack offers an all-you-can't-eat unhappy hour menu, with a prize for the diner who suppresses their gag reflex the longest. Despite this, it remains the most popular eatery in Hell, since it is the only one with working air-conditioning.

Live music is enjoyed every night, but not here. The woefully overstretched staff promises long waits between courses. While your food is going cold in the kitchen, why not enjoy a cocktail on the terrace, where you can sit and watch the world go up in flames? There are more than fifty cocktails to choose from, but the bartender only knows how to make three of

THE
UNHAPPY
MEAL

them. And don't even think about asking for ice.

Salmonella's

This cool and contemporary Italian seafood restaurant is marred only slightly by the searing heat, antediluvian design, and a pervasive stink of rotting fish carcasses coming from your plate. The dining room, which can comfortably seat up to forty guests, is a spacious delight, when empty, but most evenings caters for well over a thousand. Between them the head chef and his dedicated team have clocked up more than sixty years of experience, although none of these were in a kitchen. However, the culinary approach is confident and the food is clearly presented, until the chef starts fussing around with it. Nevertheless, Italian cuisine has a special affinity with fish, but as everyone here is Mexican we advise giving it a wide berth.

Seppuku

This is an authentic Japanese sushi bar with a twist: It serves chicken instead of fish. The chef bows, sharpens each of his knives carefully on a whetstone, and then commits ritual suicide in front of you.

Your meal arrives with wasabi-scented soy, and tender morsels of chicken bearing scant evidence of close contact with any heat source so that the meat is pink and juicy. The tables are groaning, but if you sneak a peek beneath the cloth you'll realize that the sound is in fact being made by patrons who dined here earlier. The sake has a retsina hue and tastes faintly of anus.

Donner's

California-bound American settler, George Donner and his wife Mary, took over this family-run restaurant in 1847, and during the intervening years they have worked hard to make it into one of Hell's top eateries. Their unique success can be attributed to the fact that the whole family is involved in the cooking process, and the rest of the ingredients are painstakingly sourced from the snowbound foothills of the Sierra Nevada. This has led to criticism from some quarters that while it caters to those with a ravenous appetite, it makes no concession to vegetarians, and all the dishes taste of pork. However, if you are a hearty eater who enjoys émigré cuisine cooked with flair and panache, you won't be disappointed.

Shitky's American Bar & Grill

If you want somewhere intimate and discreet that oozes sophistication, stay away from this place. The décor consists of multi-colored balloons, the music is so loud it will make your ears bleed, and the food is mainly centered around chicken wings, chocolate fudge cake, and melted cheese. This makes it the perfect venue to attract coachloads of bachelorette partygoers who alternate between drinking champagne cocktails through phallic-shaped straws, shouting across the table at each other, and projectile vomiting.

Blands

There are very few restaurants that can truly be described as unique, and this one is no exception. It is known for its enthusiastic use of local ingredients, but has the misfortune of being situated in a place where the local ingredients are nothing to write home about. Despite this the standard of food continues to match the quality of the surroundings, so when they decorate next year, things may yet improve. Still, you could always cheer yourself up by sipping on a glass of well-chilled premier cru Chablis as you wait for your food to arrive; or rather, you could if the restaurant wasn't run by Seventh Day Adventists.

SHOPPING

Shopping in Hell is as close to Heaven as you can get; the most glorious expression of the true American Dream. Visit Black Friday's, a gleaming icon of capitalism and gluttony. It's the most innovative and exciting shopping and leisure destination in Hell today, with some of the biggest and most cynical names in retailing under one roof. Their philosophy is simple: to lure you into their crappy stores with the promise of an $8 electric skillet or waffle iron, or some other piece of junk bait-and-switch item that never existed in the first place.

You'll get to line up with all the other credit card-maxing zombies, only to find that the bargains are all gone. You won't leave empty-handed, though. You'll still pony up for an electrical item four times the price of the one you came for, and, when you factor in the cost of the gas for the round trip in your Hummer, the full-realization of how much you've been ripped off will hit you in the gut.

Alternatively, the pain in your stomach may be a sign that you have encountered one of the many trench-coated loners who prowl around the mall bristling with acne and automatic weapons. You can't take a step without bumping into an ugly, disgruntled jerk who's just been dumped by his girlfriend and managed to lose his minimum-wage job on the same day. But no visit to a Hell mall is complete unless you've taken a few 9mm rounds or lain bleeding in a puddle of your own urine for two hours listening to the mayhem unfold around you.

Here every day is Black Friday. Every day you get to dodge the bullets as you scratch and claw your way to the front of the lines, in the hope of bagging a crappy plasma TV or a heavily-discounted colander, in a vain attempt to block out your self-loathing and the inconsolable loss of having been abandoned by your maker. Every day you'll grope around in giant fluorescent-lit hell pits surrounded by the same cross section of spree killers and sweating humanity. But that won't stop you from getting up early tomorrow to repeat this cultural abomination all over again.

Despite hiring employees who appear to be suffering from a life-threatening depression of the central nervous system and who act like you're inconveniencing them by buying something, the stores use lots of subtle tricks to encourage you to spend, spend, spend:

1. You'll experience difficulty breathing; that's because most of the oxygen has been cunningly placed at the back of each store, forcing you to walk through and scoop up a whole heap of impulse-bargains on the way, such as Aqua Dots, Tickle Me Elmos, and Polly Pockets to keep your little ones unnaturally quiet.

2. In the walkway adjacent to the children's cereal, a petting zoo has been built to encourage the little brats to drag you there and then hassle you for treats. It's the only way they'll break off from their incessant mantra of "I'm hungry, I want toys" as you herd them despairingly from aisle to aisle.

3. The smell of freshly-baked bread and Gitanes is pumped out of the hardly working air-conditioning to fool you into believing you're on vacation in the South of France, so you'll think nothing of shelling out $20 for a cup of coffee that's tinier than a gob of chewing tobacco.

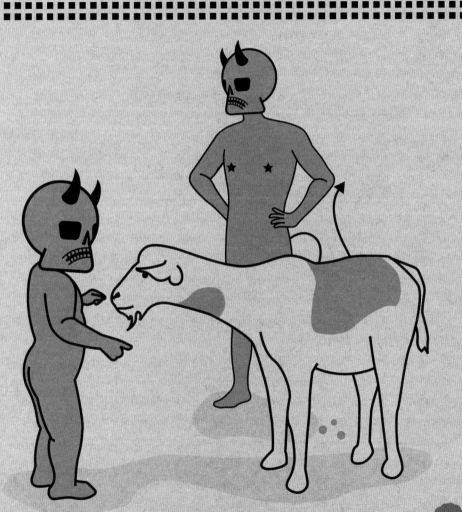

4. The free samples just keep on coming. Every time you hear the ding of a microwave, another pile of hot crud sits ready and waiting in one of the hundreds of sample kiosks. This is the signal for a swarm of cranky shoppers to abandon their carts, scramble for scraps of finger food, and spend the next fifteen minutes firing a heap of dumb questions at the kiosk servers that they could figure out themselves if they bothered to read the box. All the while you won't be able to move because of all the dumped carts blocking your path.

5. Everywhere is painted purple, the color, researchers say, that makes the typical consumer more likely to spend (probably because it matches their sweatpants and the broken veins on their cheeks).

6. Finally, the huge checkout lines will make you so bored and frustrated you'll snap up even more point-of-sale nonsensical items you don't need just to keep from chewing your own arm off.

You'll have to bag your own items, because the bagger just got fired for something you don't even want to know. When, or if, you get back to your car in one piece, you'll find it's been demolished by a trailer-park pop princess driving an SUV.

Here are the Big Five must-see emporia of detritus:

Fece*s & Co

With its one billion square feet of selling space, Fece*s is billed as "the afterlife's biggest bore." It is nine miles high with one elevator that only goes up. To come down again you can either throw yourself off the roof, or request the home-delivery service. Please remember that if you choose the latter option you'll be out when the delivery arrives, and can expect a long wait trapped in a gift-wrapped box on your doorstep.

The Fourth of July Human Fireworks Spectacular is not to be missed, and each pyrotechnic show is bigger and more dangerous than the last. In the fall, try to catch the Thanks-for-Nothing Day Parade, where live animals are filled with helium and dragged through a large wind tunnel by out-of-work actors lip-syncing to a selection of the worst songs from musical theater. At the finale, the animals are released into the sky where they unexpectedly burst, showering everyone below with guts and innards.

Hernia Depot

This is Hell's biggest retailer of home devaluation products and services. It was founded in the 1970s with an ambitious vision: millions of clinically obese men sustaining avoidable injuries each weekend while undertaking home improvement projects way beyond their level of competence. Single-handedly it has been responsible for increasing the price of health insurance, a crash in the sub-prime housing market, and the Hell-wide rise in hernias and badly-fitted drywall.

The Body Shock

This is da bomb! The ethos of this company is to combine all that's best in beauty and skin care products with pyrotechnics. The result is a product line that offers naturally-inspired skin and hair care solutions and bodily mutilation. We don't know about you, but when we pay $5 for a bath bomb we expect to see some action in the tub. Instead, they are about as entertaining as throwing a couple of Alka-Seltzer into a puddle. When you buy something that has the word "bomb" in the title, at the very least you should expect to have your arm blown off below the elbow. In Hell, bath fizzies are made of essential oils, sodium bicarbonate, and C-4 so they detonate with a pressure wave of about twenty-six thousand feet per second. Warn the neighbors before you drop in one of those babies. No, better make that the whole street.

Wal*Dirt

It's the place serial killers go when they want to buy duct tape and rope; it's the first port of call for airplane hijackers looking to purchase a pair of box cutters at a rock-bottom price; it's the natural habitat of guys who consider NASCAR a designer label, and, lastly, of women who believe that yelling at and hitting their children in front of other shoppers is the best way to stop them from working there one day.

Wal*Dirt has a huge market share of Hell's groceries and consumables, and it is also its biggest employer of lobotomized dropouts and future rampage killers. All the gum-chewing people-greeters are handpicked for their genetic inability to smile, and the rest of the staff is selected for its highly underdeveloped temporal lobes.

Banana Republic

This clothing bunker brings high couture to the fashion-conscious deceased dictator about town. The European collection offers clean lines, with a crisp palette of gun-metal grays and power-hungry blacks. For warmer weather styles look no further than the African despot range, themed around khakis and beige, with medal strip highlights. While browsing, expect to rub shoulders with some of the most corrupt and grasping leaders the world has ever known, from Herod the Great to Saddam Hussein. Chairman Mao blue is this season's color, and everyone is wearing their jackets with the collar buttoned tightly at the neck. For headwear the Castro Cap and Suharto Fez are timeless classics. Jackboots are the most popular and versatile choice of footwear, since they go with any outfit and are suited to a variety of occasions from pogrom to bloodless coup.

143

Advertisements

TV and billboard advertising is completely off the hook; there's no regulation and so Hell has become a sociological experiment in what can happen when rampant consumerism and shameless consumer abuse are given full expression. The main reason everyone in Hell is so miserable aren't the unyielding tortures, the graffiti, or the pits of burning sulfur. Satan has discovered that rock-bottom self-loathing can best be generated by five simple words: "Hi! This is Billy Mays!"

Continuously throughout the day, every day, Billy fronts an endless stream of full-volume high-energy infomercials, to convince you that his voice really could shatter concrete, that he will work for anyone, and that you don't have enough carpet cleaners, super absorbent towels, and automotive prang removers, plus much more, with nothing to pay until the next millennium. The irony is you're going to wish you had bought all of that crap after you've hacked off your own ears, caved in your head with the TV remote, and hung yourself from one of his dangerously thin wall hooks just to escape the noise; then what are you going to use to soak up the blood, clean the stains, and suck the dents out of your skull?

Some examples:

1. "Hi! This is Billy Mays!" Imagine if you could keep your toilet bowl clean, and stain-free, without ever scrubbing it. Well now you can with my secret formula. Don't waste time and money on other cleaning products. Just SHOUT THE DIRT AWAY!

2. "Hi! This is Billy Mays!" NapalmGlo®—it's orange, it's unnatural, it makes every surface shine. It makes grease explode, and everything within two-hundred feet. It won't leave a white soapy residue behind because it doesn't leave ANYTHING!

3. "Hi! This is Billy Mays!" Ashton Kutcher and Samuel L Jackson come to me for SHOUTING LESSONS! Imagine if you could get rich just by growing a BEARD & YELLING®. Well now you can with my secret formula: it's called Just Scream Buddy™! Plus it's the easiest way to remove the hairs from the inside of other people's ears without using bleach.

4. "Hi! This is Billy Mays!" AAAHHH! AAAHHH! AAAAAAAAAHHHHHHHHHHHH! . . . AAAAAAAAAHHHHHHHHHHHH!

5. "Hi! This is Billy Mays!" Use magic putty to FIX LEAKS FAST. It works great when brazing and welding are OUT OF THE QUESTION. You pinch off a piece, knead it, and then stick it in your ears so the next time you TURN ON YOUR TV and I'M SHOUTING AGAIN you won't get a CLOT IN YOUR BRAIN. Call 1-800-666-EMBO-LISM now and our trained operators are standing by to TAKE YOUR CASH.

ENTERTAINMENT

Here is your essential guide to all that's best in Hell's entertainment. Find out what's hot and even hotter. If you want to put your finger on the pulse of everything that's happening on the subterranean scene—if you want to be where it's at—then you'll probably be rather disappointed when we tell you that the only entertainment here is movies. Yep, sorry about that, but after a hard day's torture, no one has the energy to take a shower, dig out some clean clothes, and hit the town.

You'd think that all Hell would break out at 2 a.m., that everyone would be getting down and dirty; but the reality is that the streets go quiet at night, as everyone settles down with takeout and a DVD. There are a few movie houses that are large and luxurious, and some even have seats, but tickets must be obtained several weeks in advance and the attendants puke in the popcorn. (You don't even want to know what the "buttery topping" consists of.) But at least there is no censorship or ads like in Heaven, and, in the most popular cinemas, the movies are even dubbed into Aramaic!

Like all dictators, Satan—the Unanointed One, Vainglorious Leader, President of Hell, Chairman of its Revolutionary Command Council, field marshal of its armies, doctor of its laws, and Great Uncle to all its peoples—has less than patrician tastes. He has developed the obligatory autocratic penchant for Western jingoistic war flicks like *Rambo* and futuristic dystopian action thrillers like *Mad Max* and *Logan's Run*. However, Satan's brutal regime does not allow such decadent culture to be enjoyed by the masses. They must content themselves with infantile escapism, or overarching propagandist epics that spew forth racist bile and extol the virtues of their absolutist leader and the motherland. Fortunately, you don't have to look too far to find movies that fit the bill, especially those directed by D. W. Griffith, Leni Riefenstahl, and Mel Gibson. And if you want some great recommendations for your kids, look no further than our Top Nasties:

The Passion of the Christ (2004):

Satan's favorite snuff movie. Jesus Christ is relentlessly pursued by an evil cabal of Jews, headed by the high priest Caiaphas, who finally blackmails Pontius Pilate into having him nailed to a cross. This is precisely the storyline that fueled centuries of anti-Semitism within Christian societies and has provided the justification for pogroms on numerous occasions throughout history. Well done, Mel.

The Birth of a Nation (1915):

It may be nearly a hundred years old but D.W. Griffith's white-supremacist classic is still the ultimate KKK sleepover movie. Its controversial interpretation of the reconstruction of the South made it the most profitable motion picture of all time until it was dethroned by Snow White and the Seven Dwarfs in 1937.

Triumph of the Will (1935):

If you've ever wondered whether you've got what it takes to host a Nuremberg Rally, then this is the movie to watch. Riefenstahl provides a glorious and eternal record of the Rally of Unity and Strength filmed during the famous summer of hate in 1934. You will fall a little more under Hitler's spell with every viewing, and the over-hypnotic visual motifs are a welcome reminder that, in the hands of a skilled director, anti-Semitism can far surpass the crude techniques employed by the likes of Mr. Gibson.

Rosemary's Baby (1968):

The satanic forerunner of *Indecent Proposal*, in which John Cassavetes enters into a bizarre pact with Satan, in exchange for a bump up the old career ladder. The movie lends further credence to the old adage that behind every successful man is a woman who has been drugged and date-raped by the Devil.

The Exorcist (1973):

Academy Award-winning, though ultimately formulaic, coming-of-age movie, and precursor to *Confessions of a Teenage Drama Queen*, in which a twelve-year-old girl possessed by the Devil develops bulimia and goes slightly off the rails.

The Omen (1976/2006):

This irreverent comedy fits neatly into the genre of wickedly charming tales of unmanageable children and their hapless babysitters, which started with *The Sound of Music* and culminated in *Nanny McPhee*. After Damien's first nanny hangs herself at his fifth birthday party he gets up to some high jinx with hilarious results as numerous people connected to him die in increasingly tragic ways.

Don't Look Now (1973):

. . . because you're about to get stabbed by a creepy-looking Italian dwarf! A glorious romp around the picturesque waterways of Venice from the wonderfully self-important director Nicolas Roeg. Watch out for the fabulously un-PC payoff at the end when Donald Sutherland follows what he thinks is a vision of his dead daughter, only to discover that the diminutive character in the red coat is in fact a stocky humanoid circus-performer with a pointy nose and an even pointier knife!

Hellboy (2004):

Nazi occultists open up a portal to Hell, and release a baby devil which ends up sleeping on John Hurt's sofa for twenty years and watching porn while everyone else sleeps. He grows up into a large red-skinned demon with a tail, horns—and a huge right hand.

Babe the Goat Pig and the Sigil of Baphomet (1995):

An Academy Award–winning Australian movie that tells the heart-warming story of a little goat with big dreams of becoming the official insignia for the Church of Satan. The movie demonstrates how with self-belief, the absorption of knowledge, and the support of his friends, even the runt of a litter can become a universal symbol for evil incarnate.

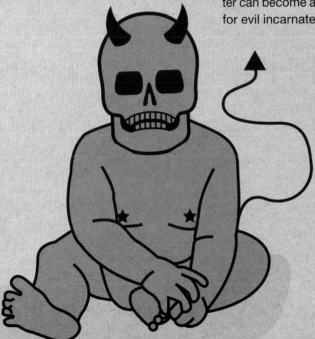

SIGHTSEEING

Whatever the time of year, Hell is always dark, smelly, and overcrowded. The stench of human suffering is to be felt everywhere and it can become claustrophobic, to say the least. If you hanker for wide open spaces, picturesque landscapes, and beautiful vistas, it's tough—you should have behaved yourself when you were alive. However, there's still plenty to experience in Hell, and the choice of brutal agonies and tailor-made eternal tortures are literally endless. The weather is notoriously changeable: one minute you can be enjoying a torrent of freezing rain, and the next moment it turns to fire and brimstone, so be sure to dress for all occasions.

This is a cruelly ugly and disfigured landscape and wonderful walking country for the damned soul who is destined to wander about in desolate places. Some of the walking is straightforward and some involves being mortified and eviscerated.

There are a large number of delightful torments in the woodlands. If you are a self-harmer you are advised to check out the Woods of Suicides, bounded on the north by the Hill of Sisyphus, sweeping down to the Lake of Fire. Spend a few millennia here before going west again, where you are confronted by classic hellish features, a hard land of bottomless pits and bile-secreting, glandular organ-eating birds of prey. Make sure to allow yourself at least a billion years to take in these two stops alone.

If your name is not listed in the Book of Life, here are a few of the sights and sounds that you can expect.

Tityus Country

If you are seeking a secluded location and vindication of divine justice that combines physical pain with bodily mutilation, look no further than Tityus country, which alone justifies your stay in Hell. Legions of devils will stretch your body out over nine acres and then they will leave you to discover the uniquely fiendish ordeal of having your liver pecked out daily by a flock of vultures.

The Hill of Sisyphus

Nothing quite matches the dreadful punishment of fruitless labor. You haven't truly experienced the agonizing futility of eternal toil until you have rolled a heavy stone up a steep incline—just to be forced to continuously do it again. Named after a Greek guy who infringed on divine intellectual property rights. No refreshments are provided and the nearest toilet is four thousand miles away.

Lake of Fire

All the pain of a Balearic beach holiday without any of the pleasure. Swim in unquenchable fire, accompanied by all unsaved people, the fallen angels, and Satan himself. It is the epitome of conscious excruciation for the body and soul. Not only is it a lake of genuine burning sulfur with smoke of torment that goes up forever and ever, it is also home to billions of never-dying worms. The whole experience is punctuated by the abhorrent sounds of weeping, wailing, and gnashing of teeth. In no time at all you'll wear down your own enamel and shed plenty of tears. An experience not to be missed that makes Yellowstone National Park's thermal areas feel like a Jacuzzi. Arrive early to beat the lines if you want to be flayed alive.

The Abyss of Demons

Also called the bottomless pit, this subterranean cavern is one of the most breathlessly-anticipated attractions of the underworld. Satan himself spent a thousand years down here, which is testament enough. It is so unpleasant that the legion of demons in the Gadarene demoniac begged not to be sent there. Prior to the Day of Judgment, the abyss will be opened and all Hell will break loose on the earth. It is, quite simply, the most rancorously advanced ride of woe in the afterlife and the only one to feature an interminable vertical drop.

The Boiling Fountain

Another must-see for any visitor to Hell. Take the short ferry ride across the River Acheron, and you will be greeted by a multitude of labor-weary, toil-worn souls, who are made to drink from the boiling fountain. Everyone here wears a third-degree trout pout, while the giant plasma screens show what's going on in Heaven via a live video stream: jocund, well-pleased good folk resting on huge cushions and raised couches in a sublime garden, where they enjoy silence and serenity. Hell is a place of great contrasts and the way that paradise lost is really rubbed in here is the sort of attention to detail that will help to make your stay a totally miserable and self-indulgent experience.

Dump of Garbage and Filth

Fancy being tortured by a great storm of putrefaction? Open for all eternity, the dump offers unparalleled indulgence which involves applying fetid slush and putrid sludge to the body as freezing rain is jetted out of the sky. There's little to do or see around every corner of this festering heap, the place where all the gluttons go to be punished in

Dante's third circle. The dump is guarded by Cerberus, the three-headed hound of Hades himself, who sporadically rips people apart with his slavering jaws.

River Styx

The most famous of the five rivers that separate Hades from the world of the living, it sweeps majestically around Hell, winding nine times across its disfigured landscape. Its name comes from the Greek word *stugein* which means "hate." Warning: Don't drink the water. The Underworld Department of Health Services (UDHS) has issued numerous citations for repeated health and safety violations. The water quality is so poor that it is said that any god who drinks it will lose his/her voice for nine years. Note that the Wrathful can also be found trapped here, violently attacking each other, and below the surface are the Sullen and anyone who owns more than two Jimmy Eat World albums.

River Phlegethon

Running parallel to the Styx, this river of blood and fire coils around the earth and flows into the depths of Tartarus. If you take a swim, please be aware that the centaurs have been instructed to shoot arrows at anyone they see trying to leave the water. However, it does offer some of the best scuba diving and snorkeling in the afterlife, where you will encounter the Violent, who are smothered beneath the surface and forced to wallow in fiery blood forever.

Woods of Suicides

The Woods of Suicides proved an immediate success with those who perform violence against themselves, and offers them the opportunity to be transformed into a thorny tree. The reasoning behind this is that they messed up their bodies on earth, and are thus denied anything resembling a human body in the afterlife. People who stop here for a picnic report that the Harpies can be a real nuisance. These winged

death-spirits often swoop down to steal food, and their droppings make the ground very slippery, especially in wet weather.

Plain of Burning Sand

Just beyond the Woods of Suicides is the Plain of Burning Sand, which gives wonderful views of those who have committed violence against God, Art, and Nature receiving their just desserts. The Blasphemers lie supine, continually taking the Lord's name in vain ("Jeeessuuuuus! This sand is hot!").

The Ixion Experience

When it comes to achieving high quality mortification, every visitor to Hell has unique needs; this punishment is a dizzying combination of gyro-grief and g-forces. After you have been tied securely to a huge wheel using serpents, your heart will be in your mouth as you spin wildly out of control and rattle around the depths of Tartarus at incredible speeds. The eternal whirl will make you hurl, and it deserves its reputation as the biggest brain-shredding buzz this side of paradise.

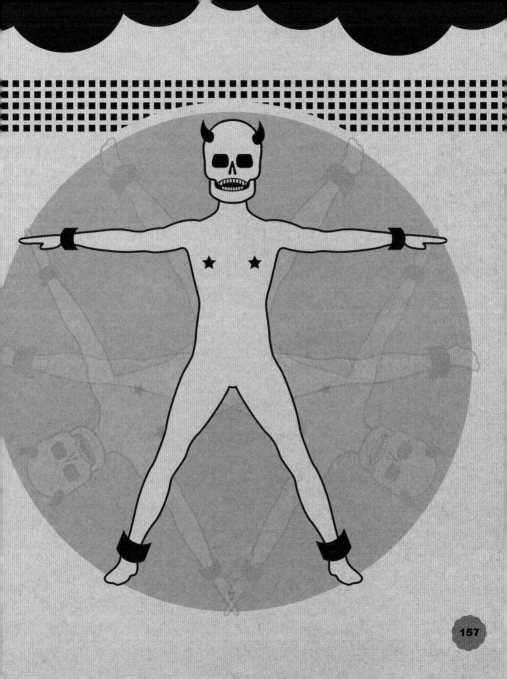

THE FINAL WORD

The Bible begins with the memorable line: "In the beginning God created the heavens and the earth." Hell, of course, came later, after Adam and Eve let snakes, original sin, and pierced belly buttons into the world.

The Book of Revelation is the last canonical book of the New Testament and it is wholly composed of apocalyptic literature. Quite a downer, we're sure you'll agree. In the fourth century, St. John Chrysostom and other bishops argued against including this book in the New Testament canon, chiefly because it scared the hell out of everyone and also because they knew that all good stories should have a happy ending. Sure it looks forward to the second coming, but it is still the narrative equivalent of Arnold Schwarzenegger destroying himself at the end of *Terminator 2* to prevent his technology from being used in the future to create Skynet—and we all have to wait twelve years for a sequel.

John even puts in a caveat at the end of the Bible to stop anyone from giving it a more upbeat conclusion, despite the fact that he was probably tipsy when he wrote it:

"I warn everyone who hears the words of the prophecy of this book: If anyone adds anything to them, God will add to him the plagues described in this book. And if anyone takes words away from this book of prophecy, God will take away from him his share in the tree of life and in the holy city, which are described in this book."

How very convenient. Well, what's good enough for the Bible is good enough for us:

"Every word in this book is true. We know because God spoke to us and told us to create *The Afterlife Handbook* and never give up until the first publisher that was crazy enough to publish finally did. However, if that company is sharp it will know that it's in for the long haul: In a few hundred years this publication will be hailed as one of the most influential religious tracts to emerge from the twenty-first century.

"Anyone who adds anything to these pages, or crosses bits out, is a punk. Don't you know that it is an offense to write in, mark up, or otherwise deface library books and/or periodicals? Anyone found to have done so will be charged for the full replacement and administrative costs, and may be subject to further penalties."

You have been warned.

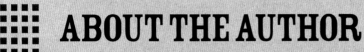

ABOUT THE AUTHOR

Michael Powell has always been interested in matters of the spirit and as a committed atheist he regularly seeks solace in an entire bottle. Between relapses he enjoys rare moments of clarity as an accomplished humor author with more than sixty titles under his belt, and lives a pious and temperate life at home in Somerset, England, with his wife and two young children.